From Lew Alcindor
to Kareem Abdul-Jabbar

From Lew Alcindor to Kareem Abdul-Jabbar

JAMES HASKINS

Illustrated with photographs

REVISED EDITION

Lothrop, Lee & Shepard Co., New York
A Division of William Morrow & Co., Inc.

Title page photo: *United Press International Photo*

Copyright © 1972, 1978 by James Haskins

Printed in the United States of America.

First Edition   1   2   3   4   5   6   7   8   9   10

Library of Congress Cataloging in Publication Data

Haskins, James (date)
    From Lew Alcindor to Kareem Abdul-Jabbar, Revised Edition

    Includes index.
    SUMMARY: A biography of the star basketball player.
    1. Abdul-Jabbar, Kareem, 1947-   —Juvenile
literature.   2. Basketball players—United States—
Biography—Juvenile literature.   [1. Abdul-Jabbar, Kareem,
1947-   2. Basketball players]   I. Title.
GV884.A24H37   796.32'3'0922   [92]   78-1016
ISBN 0-688-41821-X
ISBN 0-688-51821-4 lib. bdg.

TO LOLITA ALI

Contents

ACKNOWLEDGMENTS

I wish to make grateful acknowledgment to Joe Jares and Jack Olsen of *Sports Illustrated* from whose articles I obtained much of my material. Grateful acknowledgment also goes to the other authors and periodicals that provided material not otherwise available.

Thanks also to Donnie Brown, who conceived the idea for this biography, and to my researcher, Kathy Benson, who proved indispensable.

J. H.

1

A Large, Economy-size Child

"MY EARLIEST MEMORY IS OF SITTING ON THE GRASS IN Central Park. It was bright and sunny, airy. I was about three. My mother was with me. I was running around on this bright green carpet of grass, still getting used to the fact that I was the large, economy-size child. My parents tell me I was 22½ inches long and 12 pounds 11 ounces in weight when I was born, but I don't remember back that far. I do remember playing in the grass of Central Park around 110th Street when I was three. And I remember a ball. In my earliest memory I was playing with a ball."

Think of Lew Alcindor and you think immediately of his large size and a ball—a basketball—for Lew Alcindor is the tallest and one of the greatest basketball players in the history of sports. But Lew Alcindor is much more than a very tall, very good basketball player. He is also an intelligent, sensitive young black man who, for one reason or another—height, race, religion, background—has nearly all his life been "different." His high school basketball coach used to describe him as "a minority of one."

Ferdinand Lewis Alcindor, Jr., was not always aware of his differentness. Born in New York City on April 16, 1947, he was just like many other little boys. He did not have any brothers or sisters, but he was never lonely. He could explore the apartment, help his mother cook and clean, and spend hours watching the people and traffic out on Seventh Avenue. When she was not busy, Lew's mother would read to him, and Lew learned to love books at a very early age. After Lew learned how to read he would spend hours reading by himself.

Lew's father plays the trombone, and even when Lew was a baby Mr. Alcindor would take him along to the Elks Club at Fifth Avenue and 126th Street where he met other jazz musicians for long jam sessions. Mr. Alcindor would park Lew's carriage near where he and the other musicians played, and for hours Lew would be enveloped in the sounds of jazz. It is no wonder that Lew is an avid jazz fan today.

Mr. Alcindor worked as a bill collector for a furniture company, but music was the career he really wanted. He took courses at the Juilliard School of Music, where he studied conducting, trombone, and piano. He was graduated from Juilliard in 1952. Even though Lew was only five at the time, his mother took him to the graduation ceremonies and he remembers them vividly—the large auditorium, the music, all the people. Several other relatives attended also, and Lew knew that this was a very proud moment for the whole family.

When he was a little older, he too would understand and feel the Alcindor family pride. His father would tell him about his ancestors in Trinidad, an island in the West Indies, and about the place named Alcindor Trace in the Balandra district of Trinidad. It was Lew's grandfather who had left Trinidad for New York many years before and brought the Alcindor name to the United States. Lew often wished he could have seen his grandfather, who died before he was born. His father said Lew had gotten his height from his grandfather, who was 6'8" tall and towered over other men. He had long, flowing hair and a fierce-looking handlebar mustache and he spoke Yoruba, the dialect of his ancestors in Nigeria, Africa. Lew's grandmother was still living, and he loved to visit her and listen as she told stories of the family in her soft, musical voice that still held many traces of the Trinidad dialect.

For Lew, it was hard to imagine Trinidad, no matter how often his father and grandmother described it. Trinidad, they said, was an island of palm trees and sandy white beaches surrounded by ocean bluer than the sky. In Lew's neighborhood around Seventh Avenue and 111th Street in New York City, there were only a few scraggly trees, although Central Park was not far away. The rest was stone and concrete. When Lew was still very young his father decided the neighborhood was becoming too dirty and unsafe, and he moved his family to an area called Inwood in the northern part of Manhattan. Inwood had parks and rolling hills and lots of green grass and trees. From his bedroom window on the fifth floor of the Dyckman housing project, Lew would look out on Fort Tryon Park and wonder if Trinidad looked something like that. Already he was different, although he didn't realize it. Most black children in Manhattan can see nothing but alleys and other buildings from their windows, and few have bedrooms of their own.

Also unlike most black children in Manhattan, Lew had mainly white friends. Many more whites than blacks lived in the Dyckman housing project and Lew attended a private Catholic boys' school, St. Jude's, where, in a school comprising grades one through eight, he was one of only two black boys. Lew sometimes had trouble getting along with the other children because of his height—he was taller than the children his age but too young to play with the older children—but at that young age neither Lew nor the other children thought about their racial differences.

At that age Lew did not understand what it meant to be black in America. He was too young to wonder why his father had gone to work for the New York City Transit Authority after graduating from music school instead of getting a job conducting an orchestra, which is what he had wanted to do. Lew was too young to understand that there were few opportunities for a black man to become a conductor no matter how talented he was.

Indeed, it was not until he was about nine years old that Lew began to wonder why he and his father had to go down to Harlem to have their hair cut. When he asked his father why, he was told that the barbers in Inwood either might not cut their hair properly or might not want to cut their hair at all. Lew thought about his father's answer for a long time, but he did not really understand what it meant for him as a black boy. That understanding would come to him, as it does to all black children, a little at a time, starting with things like the long bus ride for a haircut.

Lew was in third grade when he first became aware that he was different from the white children. When he was in fourth grade, he realized that he was different from many other black children. By the time Lew was ready to enter fourth grade both his parents were working and that meant no one would be home when he returned from school. One day, Lew's parents explained to him that they did not want him home alone after school and so he would not be returning to St. Jude's in the fall. Instead, he would go to Holy Providence, a Catholic school in Pennsylvania.

Lew, who was unhappy about going to school so far away from home, was even more unhappy when he arrived at Holy Providence. While at St. Jude's there had been only one other black boy besides himself, at Holy Providence there were only a few white boys. Most of the students were Indian and black boys from the ghettos of Philadelphia and Washington, D.C., and they were unlike any children Lew had ever known before. They were tough, they used words he had never heard, and they seemed always to be fighting. They teased and played tricks on the new boys, and because Lew was shy and not used to fighting they decided he was a sissy. They made jokes about his height—at nine he was 5'4" and the second-tallest boy in a school that went up to eighth grade—and soon they were also calling him "bookworm" and "teacher's pet."

Lew had loved books almost as far back as he could remember, and by the time he entered Holy Providence he read very well. The nuns at the school soon discovered his skill, and one day he was asked to read aloud in front of the seventh-grade class to show the older boys how they should be reading. It would have been bad enough to be held up as an example to his fellow fourth-graders, but it was much worse to be held up as an example to boys three years older than he. After that he was teased unmercifully.

Lew was very lonely and unhappy until basketball season came. Then, suddenly, the other boys stopped making jokes about Lew's height and started picturing him on a basketball court. One day a group of older boys asked him to play basketball with them.

Lew did not know much about basketball. His father, who was very athletic, had taught him a great

This picture, taken on February 6, 1957, is believed to be of Lew. He did not get to play very much during his one basketball season at Holy Providence and he did not score a single point in regular game play, but from then on basketball was the game for him.

Bucks County Courier Times, Bucks County, Pennsylvania

deal about swimming, track, and handball, and Lew had won several medals and trophies for swimming, ice-skating, and Little League baseball. But when it came to basketball, Lew's father had only taught him how to dribble. The other boys at Holy Providence told him that it did not matter; they would teach him.

Their basketball court was the school playground and their hoop was a peach basket tied to the top of a metal swing frame. Their rules were their own, and theirs was a rough-and-tumble brand of basketball. When Holy Providence played another school, Lew, four years younger than the other members of the team, rarely got a chance to play. But from that time on, basketball was *the* game for him. He loved the speed of the game, the pounding down the court toward the basket, the thrill of putting the ball through the hoop despite the waving arms and jabbing elbows, the shout that went up each time a basket was made. Even though Lew didn't get to play very much, he had the consolation that the same boys who just a few weeks before had called him bookworm and teacher's pet had *asked* him to be on the team.

Soon Lew had adopted the rough speech and manner of the other boys and had become good friends with many of them. Even after basketball season ended they continued to practice, and Lew talked excitedly about developing his skill so he would get to play in more games next season. But Lew did not play another basketball season at Holy Providence. When the year ended he returned home so greatly changed that his parents decided against sending him back to the school. His rough speech and manners did not please his parents, who made it very clear that he had better readopt the old ways quickly.

It was not hard for Lew to change back, at least outwardly—in his home environment he knew the rules and how he was supposed to act—but he missed the friends he had made at Holy Providence, and he had learned things from them that he could not forget. He had realized that some black children were very different from him and had learned that to them the world was unfriendly—something to mistrust, something to fight. He had begun to feel as they did, and although that unfriendly world seemed far away once he was back in Inwood, he now knew it was there.

When Lew returned to St. Jude's that fall he was much more aware of being one of the very few black boys in the school, and although he continued to be best friends with several white boys, he began to find more in common with the other black boys. He spent a great deal of time playing basketball. By that time he was only one-half inch shorter than the tallest boy, an eighth-grader, on St. Jude's basketball team, and although he was clumsy and still not a very good player, he was put on the team because of his height. Again he spent most of the season on the bench, but he came to love basketball even more and determined to spend as much time as necessary to learn to play well.

That summer he ran track to develop his speed, and it paid off in an unexpected way. One day he had parked his bike and was walking near the Harlem River Drive when he looked up to see two boys speeding off on their bicycles carrying his English racer between them. Lew chased them for two miles before they became frightened enough to drop his bicycle and escape.

By the time he entered sixth grade, Lew was six feet tall. The story goes that on the first day his teacher looked up from her desk and asked him, "Why aren't you sitting down?" "I *am* sitting down," Lew is supposed to have replied. The other boys would laugh at such incidents but Lew rarely joined in the laughter. He was very self-conscious about his height—even more so now that he was playing basketball. No matter how hard he practiced, he was still clumsy and missed many shots. He was aware that other people could not understand why such a tall boy could not play well, and he was very uncomfortable out on the court while people were watching him. In a way, he was almost glad that he did not play in many games in sixth grade either.

Farrell Hopkins, who coached every sport at St. Jude's, saw the boy's self-consciousness and realized that it was hindering his development as a basketball player. He saw that Lew had the potential to be a fine player and set out to help him build up both his skill and his self-confidence. He persuaded Lew to practice his shots until he perfected them, starting with the shots that most embarrassed Lew to miss, like the lay-up. To give Lew as much time as possible to practice alone, Hopkins arranged for Lew to continue to practice in the gym after regular practice was over. While the other boys left at five o'clock, Lew stayed on in the gym until six or seven. Gradually, as his skill increased, Lew began to overcome his self-consciousness on the court.

At about the same time, Lew's self-consciousness about being black increased. One day in the school lunchroom he heard a white boy say, "You know, if you put charcoal on you enough days in a row and let it settle in, you'll turn black!" All the other white boys became silent at such a terrible thought. Lew became silent too, thinking, "What's wrong with being black?"

Lew could not answer the question. Ever since he was nine years old he had been aware that he was different because he was black. Now, it seemed, being black meant not only that you were different but that there was something wrong with you. At least the white boys thought so—including his friend, John Freeman. The two boys had been best friends until the sixth grade, when they had begun to drift apart and each had become more friendly with boys of his own race. Lew did not become less friendly with John because John was white; he simply found that he had more in common with the other black boys at St. Jude's. He thought John had become closer to some other white boys for the same reason.

But one day when Lew was in seventh grade John

and two of his friends came up to Lew and John said, "Hey, *Blackie*, what are you doing?" Lew was stunned. Why had John called him "Blackie?" From then on, whenever John saw him he seemed to have a new name—"Nigger," "Black Boy"; Lew could not understand the change in his one-time friend. The other white boys were soon calling him names too.

For a while, Lew dreaded going to school, for suddenly it was a strange and unfriendly place. He kept to himself, avoiding John and his white friends and willing the clock's hands to move faster so that another school day would be over and he could escape to his home and his own room. Sometimes he became angry and vowed to think twice before he became friendly with any white boys again, but he usually forgot his vow whenever one of the white boys was nice to him. More and more he and the few other black boys at St. Jude's clung together, and together they learned that there were new rules they must follow—certain unspoken rules that governed their relationship with the white boys. They might joke or play sports with the others but they could no longer confide in their white friends or talk about serious subjects with them.

Holy Providence is now an all-girls school, but the girls are just as proud as boys would be that Lew Alcindor was once a student at the school. Here Charles Duke, who coached the boys at Holy Providence in his spare time and was Lew's first coach, reads a magazine article about Lew with five Holy Providence students.

Bucks County Courier Times, Bucks County, Pennsylvania

The white boys seemed to obey the same rules, which were strictest in the boys' social life. Lew and the other black boys became very much aware that if they so much as looked at a white girl they were in for some kind of trouble.

Finding his world suddenly narrowed in this way, Lew concentrated even more on his studies and on basketball, and as there were few other black youths either at St. Jude's or in the Dyckman housing project, Lew began to go down to Harlem for friends and social life as well as for haircuts. There he made friends easily and often played basketball. Gradually his game was improving, and that year St. Jude's basketball team had a fairly good season. By then, Lew had grown to a height of 6'5" and suddenly he discovered he could touch the rim of the basket. It happened during a game, and he was so amazed that after everyone else had gone home he stayed to jump up and touch the rim thirty times before he would believe it.

He could touch the rim of the basket and he was only in seventh grade! Suddenly, Lew no longer felt the need to practice the basic basketball skills, and whenever Coach Hopkins was not around he would practice trick moves and shots, envisioning himself someday playing with the Harlem Globetrotters. He was far from being the kind of basketball player that he could be, but for the rest of his time at St. Jude's Lew found it hard to feel challenged to develop his skill further. Other players were no match for his height, which continued to increase. By eighth grade, when he was fourteen years old, he was 6'8" tall and could dunk the ball. At one away-game in eighth grade he scored 33 points, which was more than the entire St. Jude's team usually scored.

Now Lew no longer dreaded going to school. He was a celebrity at St. Jude's. Everywhere he went the students greeted him with "Good game, Lew." and "Boy, you sure showed that other team!" His relationship with most of the white students did not go much beyond casual conversation about basketball, but he didn't mind. He had his black friends, and now the white boys would think twice before they called him "Nigger."

The name Lew Alcindor was becoming known in New York City basketball circles, and soon Lew began to receive visits from high school recruiters urging him to go to the high schools they represented. They gave him free tickets to professional games, and Lew was thrilled to meet some of his greatest idols, like Elgin Baylor and Bill Russell of the Boston Celtics. The recruiters also offered scholarships to the high schools they represented, and Lew found himself able to choose among the best high schools in the area. It was all very exciting for a thirteen-year-old boy.

As his eighth-grade year wore on, Lew leaned more and more toward Power Memorial Academy in Manhattan. His friend Arthur Kenny, who lived in the Dyckman housing project, was a freshman at Power. Lew often played basketball with Arthur, who was a very gifted player, and Arthur took Lew to Power's gym to practice. Power's coach, Jack Donohue, happened to be at the gym one day while Lew and Arthur were practicing. He took one look at the 6'8" Lew and decided to offer him a full scholarship.

Power Memorial had a fine academic standing, a factor that was very important to Lew, who had not missed the honor roll since fifth grade and wanted to be an architect. It was on the subway line closest to where he lived. He had practiced in the school's gym and liked the court, and he liked Coach Donohue and knew he was a good coach. When the time came for Lew to choose a high school, he chose Power Memorial without hesitation. Only later did Lew and Arthur Kenny learn that until Donohue saw Lew, he had been planning to offer the scholarship to Arthur. Lew felt badly when he found out that he had unwittingly taken the scholarship away from his friend, but his family and Arthur himself assured him that he should not feel guilty.

Almost as soon as Lew announced his decision to go to Power, Donohue began to train him for the upcoming basketball season. Donohue had started a summer camp for boys called Friendship Farm in upstate New York and invited Lew to spend the summer before his freshman year at Power there. He would work as a dishwasher during the day in exchange for room and board, and after work he could practice his basketball skills on the outdoor courts.

Lew did not really want to go to Friendship Farm. He would much rather have remained in New York

City where he could go to Harlem and play basketball with his friends there. But he liked Donohue and realized that he would be playing basketball under him for the next four years, so he went to the camp. Once there, however, Lew regretted his decision. He was the only black boy at the camp, and the other boys would have nothing to do with him. After three of the loneliest and unhappiest weeks of his life, Lew decided he just couldn't take any more and went home. He could not help blaming Donohue for not realizing how unhappy he would be at the camp and wondered at his coach's lack of sensitivity to his feelings.

2
Far From a Normal Teen-ager

POWER MEMORIAL ACADEMY WAS A COMPLETELY NEW experience for Lew. It was far from home—nearly two hundred blocks—and Lew had to ride the crowded subway to and from school every morning and evening. The Christian Brothers of Ireland, who ran the school, were very strict, and Lew had to study harder than he ever had before. But the racial situation was not new. Blacks constituted only about five percent of the students, who were mainly Irish and Italian. As at St. Jude's, Lew was set apart, and as at St. Jude's he soon became known as a loner. Jack Donohue recalls, "I tried to tell him that he had to believe in what he was, to find pride in himself, because in everything he was a minority. He was seven feet. That's a minority for sure. And a Negro. And a Catholic. And he went to a private school. That must be the smallest minority in the world. 'Lewie,' I said, 'let's face it. You're just a minority of one.'"

Lew bided his time, waiting for basketball season to arrive. He always felt better about being a minority of one during basketball season. He was pleased to learn that he would join the varsity team immediately in-

The surprised looks on the faces of the rival team players as Lew easily hooks the ball into the basket show what a great psychological effect Lew had upon Power's opponents.

stead of spending his first year on the junior varsity, where freshmen were usually placed. He was still very awkward and his game consisted mainly of waving his long skinny arms and dunking an occasional basket, but he was a great asset to the team in other ways. Just his height was enough to make many rival players despair, and some rival team coaches would make sure their teams were back in the locker room before the Power Panthers came out to practice so the players would not have to see Lew any sooner than they had to.

Lew's effect on the other teams was a common joke at Power and among sportswriters, but Lew himself did not think it funny. He wanted to be a threat because of his skill, not just because of his height, and he stuck diligently to the strict training schedule Donohue set for him—skipping rope, playing handball, and practicing his shots for hours. There was little else for him to do at Power besides study and practice. Gradually his coordination improved, and after his freshman year he no longer could be called awkward.

That summer Lew went again to Friendship Farm. He was no happier there this time than he had been the summer before, but he stuck it out, finding escape from his loneliness and the hostility of the other boys in his concentration upon basketball. He knew he was getting better and that knowledge spurred him on.

In his sophomore year, Lew's determination and hours of practice really began to show results. He still was a great psychological asset to the team. During the pre-game warm-up he would lope out onto the court sucking a lollipop for quick energy, and begin taking shots from somewhere near the half-court line. Then he would dunk a few shots, first with his right hand and then with his left, feet firmly planted on the ground. Audible moans could be heard from the rival team. But now his great height was combined with a skill that seemed effortless, though it had taken him thousands of hours to achieve it. When he played, he stood slightly stooped and seemed almost disinterested in the game. But on defense, although he sometimes forgot to put his hands up, he blocked shot after shot and usually led the field in rebounds. On offense, when the ball came his way and he was able to make a shot, he took it and rarely missed. Rival teams put two or three men on guarding him, but he had learned to pass the ball off to his teammates, who were good players, and the Power team scored anyway. Power Memorial was undefeated in twenty-seven games that year and won the city Catholic high school championship. Lew averaged nineteen points and eighteen rebounds per game and was named to the high school All-America team. He was hailed as the most promising high school player in the country.

His picture was in national magazines. Reporters kept the telephone constantly ringing with requests for pictures and interviews. And the recruiters seemed to be around every corner, using every means they could think of to persuade him to go to the colleges they represented—even though college was more than two years away. Both Lew's parents and Coach Donohue feared that too much publicity could hurt Lew, and Donohue was worried about its effect on the rest of the team. He decided on a policy that set a precedent for dealing with recruiters and reporters who were after a promising young athlete. Lew was to dodge the recruiters as best he could and refuse to talk to them if they succeeded in cornering him. Letters from colleges were to be handed over, unopened, to Donohue. Sportswriters had to submit all their questions in writing to Donohue, and Lew was instructed to avoid all photographers. That was often easier said than done. Once Lew had to pivot down the platform of the 59th Street subway station in order to escape a determined *Life* photographer; it could have been a chase scene in a movie. Because of these precautions, Lew was able to lead a fairly normal life—at least as normal a life as a 6'8" teen-ager whose name was already famous in basketball could lead.

Compared to the lives of other boys his age, however, Lew's was far from normal. His height was the overwhelming fact of his life. He felt uncomfortable when he had to stand and talk to people—especially adults, because he towered over them. Off the court he had to bear stares and comments like "How's the weather up there?" Once, when he was thirteen, an elderly woman went up to him and poked him with her umbrella, just to see if he was real. He wore size 16D sneakers and slept in a custom-made 7'6" bed. It was easy for people to forget that he was fifteen, saving for a new bike, and now wanted to be an engineer.

The summer after his sophomore year, Lew again went to Donohue's Friendship Farm. He had been offered a job as a busboy at a Catskill Mountain resort, and the owners had wanted him so much that they had even consented to pay him two thousand dollars. But, on the advice of Donohue, Lew turned the offer down. He would have liked to take the job in the Cat-skills, but he trusted Donohue and thought that what-ever Donohue decided was best for him. So he went to Friendship Farm for the third time and spent an-other lonely summer, an outcast from the activities and friendships among the other boys. Lew tried not to blame Donohue, realizing that he meant well, but he was beginning to feel rather caged by Donohue.

It seemed to Lew that the more he played with Power Memorial and the more he scored and the more games the team won, the more Donohue tried to run his life. Lew could understand his coach's strictness about things relating to basketball, but he resented Donohue's trying to tell him what to do outside of school. Lew was particularly offended at Donohue's attempts to keep him out of Harlem where, the coach seemed to feel, Lew was in danger of meeting up with junkies and pushers and criminals. The man should have had more trust in him, Lew felt, and he should have understood that Harlem was important to both Lew's basketball and his social life. Did Donohue see him only as an athlete, and not as a human being?

Lew got an inkling of the answer to that question in his junior year. Power Memorial was playing at St. Helena's in the Bronx in what should have been an easy game. But something was wrong with the Power Panthers and by half time their lead was much smaller than it should have been. Donohue scolded the entire team severely; then he turned to Lew and said, "And you! You go out there and you don't hustle. You don't move. You don't do any of the things you're supposed to do. *You're acting just like a nigger!*"

Lew could not believe what he had heard. After Donohue was out of earshot, the two other black players on the team angrily advised Lew to go home, but he was too numb to do anything but what he could do without thinking—and that, of course, was to return to the court when the second half started. He went through the motions of playing, and Power Memorial won. After the game a happy Donohue explained to Lew that he had made the statement in order to shock Lew into playing well, but that did not make Lew feel any better. "All I could think of was how the instant you do something wrong in front of the white race you're not only a misdoer, but you're a nigger, too. They hold that word back until you slip up, and then they lay it on you like a crowbar."

That incident marked the end of Lew's trust in Donohue. The man was just using him, he declared to his mother when he told her of the incident after he got home from the game. He was so angry that he wanted to transfer to another school, even if it meant losing a year of basketball. Mrs. Alcindor was as hurt and angry as her son, but she calmed him down and advised him that transferring to another school or even showing his anger at Donohue would only hurt Lew. They would just have to swallow their pride. But there was one way to show Donohue: Jack Donohue had become famous as Lew's coach and everyone knew that he would go to the coaching staff of some college after Lew graduated. Everyone also knew that Donohue very much wanted Lew to go with him. Lew and his mother decided that night that wherever Donohue did go, Lew certainly would *not* go. Lew felt better after that. Somehow, his mother always seemed to be able to put things in a better light. His father was so often at work or had things on his mind; it was to his mother that Lew took most of his problems, and she almost always understood.

Lew, who was by now sixteen and 7′½″, finished out the season with an average of twenty-six points and eighteen rebounds a game. Power won all twenty-five games of its season and once again became New York City Catholic high school champions. But the last part of the season was not very enjoyable for Lew because of the incident with Donohue. He could not forget the coach's words, and it was hard not to reveal his anger. Other incidents with whites occurred that year—comments on the street, things that happened at school. Perhaps the incident with Donohue had made Lew especially sensitive to being black in a white society. Whatever the reasons, Lew became increasingly bitter against whites.

The summer after his junior year, Lew made up his mind that he was going to work in Harlem rather than go to Friendship Farm a fourth summer. He got a job with a New York youth organization called Harlem Youth in Action (HARYOU–ACT) as sports editor for its newspaper (by this time he had decided to become a journalist). He also attended classes in journalism there, for he was actually a trainee, just like the other youths in the program. The directors of the program were impressed by Lew and his articles, and Lew was impressed by HARYOU–ACT: "My instructor was a fine man named Al Calloway, and for the first time in my life I learned that there was an empire in Africa in the thirteenth century, that there were thriving civilizations in Ghana and Mali and places like that centuries ago. No sooner had Mr. Calloway finished telling me something like that than I'd run to the library to look it up, and sure enough, there it was in print, the true facts about my people." Lew also learned about the history of blacks in America and about their struggle for equality; and in class they discussed such black Americans as Denmark Vesey and Nat Turner, who led slave revolts, and compared their methods with those of men like Dr. Martin Luther King. Gradually Lew was acquiring a sense of his own race's history and achievements and a pride in being black.

Lew wanted to stay with HARYOU–ACT for the whole summer, learning about the history of his race with members of his race, but by the middle of the summer he was at Friendship Farm again. Donohue had visited him several times and begged him to return to the camp, and only after Lew had turned him down repeatedly did Donohue finally admit that he had used Lew's name to attract boys to the camp and that he would be in trouble if Lew was not there as promised. Lew thought it would serve Donohue right to be in trouble, but he would be his coach for another year, and anyway, Lew felt rather sorry for him. Against his better judgment, Lew went to Friendship Farm for another unhappy few weeks. He felt very guilty about leaving HARYOU–ACT. When he told Al Calloway that he was leaving, Calloway angrily reminded him that the people of New York City had an investment in him too and that he was cheating them out of it. Lew felt that Calloway was right.

At Friendship Farm, Donohue put Lew in charge of teaching basketball to eleven- and twelve-year-olds instead of washing dishes, but Lew did not enjoy the new job. Even though they were supposed to have come to the camp because of him, the white boys were unfriendly as usual. Lew was filled with resentment against Donohue for persuading him to go to the camp and with guilt about leaving HARYOU–ACT. One day, while coaching a game, he stooped down to doodle in the dirt with a stick. He drew absentmindedly, his thoughts half on the game and half on his own problems. When he looked down at the ground he was shocked. In bold letters he had printed: DEATH TO THE WHITE MAN. He thought about erasing it but didn't; he simply walked away. Someone else saw it and erased it and nothing was ever said. Lew was very relieved when he was able to leave the camp that summer.

The Harlem riots of 1964 broke out a week after Lew returned from the camp. In fact, he emerged from a subway exit right into the middle of it—a chaos

Even sitting down, Lew dwarfed his fellow students at Power Memorial Academy. Off the basketball court his great height was not an advantage, as can be seen from this picture taken of Lew's English class in his senior year.

Photograph by The New York Times

so wild and frightening that he ran and ran until he was out of it. He was frightened, but he understood why it was happening. He was black himself and had been in Harlem enough to understand how trapped and frustrated the people who lived there felt. He recalled what he had just seen—people smashing windows and throwing bottles and fighting with club-swinging police—and his fear changed to anger. "The poor people of Harlem felt that it was better to get hit with a nightstick than to keep on taking the white

man's insults forever. I could see this and I could re-
late to it, and right then and there I knew who I was,
who I had to be. I was going to be black rage per-
sonified, Black Power in the flesh. And I decided that
in my personification of Black Power and black pride,
I was no longer going to pussyfoot around the whites.
I was going to speak my mind."

It was a hard year for Lew—the year he turned
seventeen. It was a time of acute consciousness of his
race, of himself as a young black man, and of other
black people. It had started with Donohue badgering
him about going to Harlem, then calling him "nigger."
Then Lew had gone to HARYOU–ACT, and for the
first time he had learned how great and proud his race
was. He had left to save Donohue from embarrass-
ment and had been surrounded by unfriendly whites.
And then the riots broke out in Harlem—black people
rioting against white racism. He hated whites, he said,
and once, in a fit of anger, he told his mother that he
wished he did not have any white blood in him. Mrs.
Alcindor, who is very light, was deeply hurt, and it
was in his sorrow over hurting his mother that Lew
vowed to rise above hating whites.

Lew's last basketball season at Power Memorial
contained no surprises at first. Lew had perfected his
dunk shot and his own specialty, the "backward
dunk" (backward over the head), and it seemed to
all that Lew and the Power Panthers again would be
impossible to stop. Then, after nineteen straight victories that season and seventy-one straight victories

in two and a half years, Power was beaten by De-Matha High School of Hyattsville, Maryland.

DeMatha and Power had long been rivals, and to each team playing the other was the high point of the season. This time was no exception; Power Memorial had beaten DeMatha the year before and now DeMatha was determined to beat Power, or "Alcindor Tech," as the DeMatha players called the school. On the night of the game, twelve and a half thousand fans watched DeMatha players surround Lew every time the ball came his way. Two players, each 6′8″, stayed by him all the time. That sort of defense had been tried against Lew before, but never before had it worked so well. DeMatha won, 46–43. Lew, who usually averaged thirty points a game, made only sixteen that night.

DeMatha had played a fine game, but the Power players were heartbroken. Lew blamed himself for the loss, but Donohue told him if he wanted to take the blame for this game he would also have to take credit for the seventy-one wins.

Power won all its games after that, with Lew averaging thirty-three points per game, and went on to win its third straight New York City Catholic high school championship with a resounding 73–41 victory over Rice High School. In that game Lew scored thirty-two points and brought his high school career total to two thousand sixty-seven points, a New York City high school record.

Now it was time to choose a college. The recruiters

had been after Lew since his sophomore year, and he had been offered over one hundred scholarships. He could go to the best schools in the country, and not just because he was a great basketball player; he was also a fine student. His academic average in high school was eighty-five and he had scored high enough on the New York State Regents' examination to be awarded a Regents' scholarship. Of the many colleges from which he could choose, Lew liked the University of Michigan and the University of California at Los Angeles (U.C.L.A.) best. In the spring of his senior year he received an invitation to fly out to Los Angeles to see U.C.L.A. and he eagerly accepted.

California seemed to be everything that Lew had dreamed; the U.C.L.A. campus was beautiful and the people seemed very friendly. He was escorted around the campus by Mike Warren and Edgar Lacey, two black players on the U.C.L.A. team, who told him that U.C.L.A. was great for basketball, and he liked U.C.L.A.'s coach, John Wooden, immediately. After that visit, Lew was pretty certain that he wanted to go to U.C.L.A. He visited the University of Michigan and heard Cazzie Russell tell him how good the school was for the black athlete, but that did not make him forget U.C.L.A. Later, he was to wish that he had given Michigan more of a chance.

Meanwhile, Coach Donohue had been offered and had accepted a position on the coaching staff of Holy Cross in Worcester, Massachusetts, and he strongly hinted that he would like Lew to go to Holy Cross also.

Lew had long before decided not to go where Donohue went, but he consented to visit Holy Cross as a favor to the coach. Holy Cross had very few black students, but it had been arranged that one of them should talk to Lew and try to persuade him to attend the school. Little did Donohue and the Holy Cross athletic staff know that as soon as he could not be heard by the others, the black student told Lew that black students at Holy Cross were shunned by the other students and that Lew would be crazy to go there.

After the trip to Holy Cross, Lew told Donohue that he had definitely decided upon U.C.L.A. Donohue was disappointed but wished Lew well and Lew wished his coach well in return. The preceding four years had been exciting and difficult for both of them. Lew was grateful to Donohue, from whom he had learned so much, and he believed the coach had learned something from him too.

For four years people had been asking Lew where he would go to college, and the suspense built to a fever pitch that spring. Everywhere Lew went, people leaned out of taxis and ran out of stores to call out, "Where are you going? Have you decided yet?" In May, at a special press conference, Lew announced his decision and everyone's question was answered. Lew, for one, was glad the whole thing was over.

3
An Unhappy Four Years

"EVERYBODY LIVES IN DREAMS AND FANTASIES, NO MATTER what his color, and my vision of U.C.L.A. was of an idyllic place where I would play basketball, study, go to an occasional beer bust, stroll arm in arm on the campus with the chicks, enjoy long bull sessions in the dorm with the cats and, in general, live the collegiate life that I'd read about and been promised by all those guys I'd talked to on my first visit the April before. I wasn't happy about leaving my parents and my old neighborhood, but I had to face the fact that there was prejudice in New York, and there was a permanent riot situation in the Harlem that I once loved. Maybe it was better to get away from all that for a while and go out to California, where people were color-blind and a man could live his life without reference to color or race."

Or so Lew thought before he arrived at U.C.L.A. But he soon found that California and U.C.L.A. were not at all as he had envisioned them. He found that there was just as much racism in California as there was in New York. Only three days after he arrived, he was walking on campus when he heard three white students talking about him. One of them said, "Hey, is that Lew Alcindor?" And another answered, "Yeah, that's him. He's nothing but a big ———." At least in New York, Lew felt, he had known where he stood; if someone did not like him that person would tell him to his face instead of talking behind his back.

Lew had expected the U.C.L.A. students to be mature enough not to make an issue of his height, but he was the object of as many stares and comments as ever. And he considered them immature in other ways: they never seemed to study and they spent much of their time having water fights and throwing things out of windows. Quite soon, Lew felt uncomfortable around all but the American black, African, and Asiatic students. He spent most of his time with Lucius Allen, his roommate, who also played on the freshman basketball team, and with Kenneth Kelly, one of his best friends at Power. Kelly had also gone out to California, having arranged to spend one year at Santa Monica City College and then to transfer to U.C.L.A. and run on its track team. He found a room in a fraternity house near Lew's dormitory.

Lew also became very good friends with Mike Warren and Edgar Lacey, who were on the U.C.L.A. varsity and who had served as his escorts when he had visited the U.C.L.A. campus the preceding spring. Finally, Lew became very close to J. J. Johnson, a straight A student who was very proud of being black and who introduced Lew to black literature. If it had not been for these friends, Lew believes that he would not have made it through his freshman year at U.C.L.A.

With his black friends, Lew sometimes went off campus to hear jazz at the Lighthouse on Hermosa Beach or at Shelly's Manne Hole. They also often listened to Lew's jazz albums, a collection numbering some two hundred that included Thelonious Monk, John Coltrane, Charles Mingus, and Miles Davis. And, often with the strains of good jazz providing a background, Lew and his friends enjoyed one of the most important parts of college life, the discussion of new ideas. The discussions covered a wide range of subjects, but most often they were devoted to the central fact in all the boys' lives—their blackness and what it meant to be black in white America. They talked about black pride. Lew had begun to learn the history of the black race at HARYOU–ACT the summer before his senior year at Power Memorial, and at U.C.L.A. he learned much more. Every day J. J. Johnson seemed to be carrying a different book of black literature or history and Lew read many of them.

The most important of these books, to Lew, was the *Autobiography of Malcolm X*, the story of the black man who rose from a life of crime and prisons to become an important militant black leader, and who was assassinated in February of Lew's senior year at Power. In the book, Malcolm X described his own inner struggle over being black in America. He told of his hurt at being a target of white racism and of his bitterness against whites that caused him to join the

Nation of Islam, an American-based black organization preaching hatred of whites and separation of blacks from white society. Finally, he told of his trips to Asia and Africa, where the original religion of Islam is practiced by people of all colors, and of his realization that it was not the American white man who was racist so much as the American political, economic and social atmosphere as a whole. Before he was killed, Malcolm X founded an all-black organization that would work to help create a society in which there could exist honest white-black brotherhood.

As a result of reading Malcolm X's story, Lew became very much interested in black nationalism, from the "Back to Africa" movement led by Marcus Garvey in the early 1920's to the current black nationalism of LeRoi Jones. He also became interested in the religion of Islam, the one that Malcolm X had discovered in Asia and Africa. He had been a practicing Catholic all his life, but he found much more meaning in Islam than he ever had in Catholicism or Christianity. All his life he had seen people who called themselves Christians but who were bigoted and very un-Christian in much of their behavior. The people of the Islamic religion—Muslims—seemed not just to talk about brotherly love but to practice it. Lew began to read everything he could find about Islam, including its holy book, the Qu'ran, or Koran.

Meanwhile, Lew was preparing for his first U.C.L.A. basketball season. When he arrived at U.C.L.A. his game had two chief weaknesses. First, he tired too easily. Second, he tended to turn away from the basket even as the ball was leaving his hand, and thus was not always in a position to get the rebound if he missed. In order to help Lew overcome these weaknesses, U.C.L.A. coach John Wooden got Jay Carty, a former basketball star for Oregon State University who was then studying for a doctorate at U.C.L.A., to work with Lew. To improve Lew's stamina, Carty planned a training program which included having Lew jump up and touch the line of the backboard one and a half feet above the basket fifteen times in a row. And to overcome what was called Lew's "fade-away jump shot habit," Carty devised a dunk shot drill that Lew went through every day. In addition, Carty guarded Lew in practice games, playing him hard so he would get used to the rougher college game.

Carty's training program and Lew's hard work produced fine results. In his first college game, Lew led the U.C.L.A. freshman team to a 76–60 win—over National Collegiate Athletic Association (NCAA) champions, the U.C.L.A. *varsity!* Three games later, Lew scored forty-eight points and set a new U.C.L.A. freshman single-game scoring record. By that time the freshman games, which were played before the varsity games and which usually attracted only a small audience, were being called "Super Lew's Early Show" and attracting some eight thousand fans a night. People in basketball circles were declaring that college basketball had entered "the Alcindor Era"; and because Lew could dunk the ball without leaving his feet, the

NCAA had to ban the dunk shot! Despite all the excitement over him, Lew himself was not very excited. He
rarely felt challenged that season and hoped playing
on the varsity team would not be so easy.

Of course newspaper sports columns and sports
magazines were full of stories of Lew—anything about
him was newsworthy—and reporters and sportswriters
were very annoyed that, just as during his high school
career, Lew would not grant interviews. During his
freshman year, whenever a reporter tried to catch up
with him Lew just walked faster, calling back over his
shoulder, "Freshmen are not allowed to talk to reporters."

Although Lew insists that the rule against granting
interviews was Coach Wooden's idea, the press inter-
preted it as Lew's idea and blamed him for it. It is
certain that Lew did not want to talk to the reporters.
Some of his critical comments about U.C.L.A. and
Californians had leaked to the press, and Lew was not
very popular with the local reporters anyway. It was
not surprising that they began to describe him in their
articles as moody and surly. Reading such descriptions
of himself upset Lew, and this criticism, combined
with his disappointment with U.C.L.A. and its students, created a great deal of pressure for him. He was
very glad to go home for Christmas.

At home Lew was able to relax, and in the warm
family atmosphere his resentment against the white
students and reporters ebbed away. He returned to

U.C.L.A. in a much better mood, willing to give California and its whites another chance.

Soon after he returned from New York, Lew began to date a white co-ed at U.C.L.A. The two realized that their dating would cause comment and avoided public places as much as possible, but word soon got around anyway. Suddenly male students who had hardly spoken to Lew before made a point of asking Lew about his girl. Suddenly the girl began to receive anonymous phone calls from people who called her a "nigger lover," and visits from friends wanting to have "heart-to-heart" talks with her. Both were under great pressure and finally Lew decided that their friendship just was not worth it. He told the girl that he thought it best to end the relationship.

Lew was very angry about having to stop seeing a girl he liked just because she was white and he was black and others could not understand that they were simply two human beings who enjoyed each other's company. He knew he had not escaped the racial barrier by going to California, but the incident was one more proof that no matter where he went in America he would not escape racial prejudice.

Lew was very lonely after that. Basketball season was over. All he really had left were his friends, and he was not satisfied to spend night after night with them. So once more he drew into himself, pushing into the back of his mind everything but his basketball practice and his courses—and his study of Islam. More

and more, his regular studies at U.C.L.A. were overshadowed by his reading on the black race and on the
religion of Islam.

That summer, back in New York and away from the
pressures of U.C.L.A., Lew took the kind of job he
had long wanted—with the music division of Columbia
Pictures Screen Gems. He tried to learn as many
aspects of the recording business as possible and began
to understand how the musical effects he had heard
on his jazz albums had been produced. During his
lunch hours, he learned to play the saxophone. He
enjoyed himself thoroughly, and even consented to
talk to the reporters who, it seemed, followed him
everywhere he went. But even there he could not
escape his differentness. One day a woman walked
into a room in which he was standing and screamed at
the sight of such a gigantic figure.

Lew saved a great deal of the money he earned from
his job at Screen Gems and at the end of the summer
he paid $1,100.00 for a 1958 Mercedes, his first car.
He drove it to California that fall and was to be grateful for it many times during his remaining three years
at U.C.L.A. Because of it he was able to move off
campus, and he was very glad to leave the eight-
hundred-student dormitory and rent an apartment in
Santa Monica with Edgar Lacey. He could also take
long drives whenever he was lonely or upset; somehow, he felt better just knowing he could go anywhere
he wanted whenever he wanted. He stopped eating in
the crowded student cafeteria and arranged to take

his meals in a small fraternity house where there were only thirty-five to watch him. Yes, this would be a much better year. He could train for his first varsity basketball season at U.C.L.A. with nothing else to worry about but his courses.

Lew had been looking forward to playing with Edgar Lacey, who was a junior that year, but Lacey was unable to play that season because of a knee injury. Without Lacey, the U.C.L.A. team was one of the youngest in NCAA competition, consisting of four sophomores and a junior, Mike Warren. Nevertheless, U.C.L.A. was predicted to win the NCAA championship almost entirely because of Lew, and Lew soon proved that such predictions were well founded.

In his first varsity game, Lew astonished both the audience and the rival University of Southern California team. He seemed to cover half the court in three or four bounding strides, and he moved not only quickly but gracefully. The most spectacular play of the game occurred near the end of the first half. Junior Mike Warren threw the ball high toward the basket and Lew, with perfect timing, leaped up, caught the ball, and with both hands above the basket stuffed it through. He made twenty-three baskets in thirty-two tries and ten out of fourteen foul shots to set a new U.C.L.A. single-game scoring record of fifty-six points.

That game was the only one in which Lew's opponents used the usual man-to-man defense against him. In fact, everything legal was tried against Lew

Early in his first varsity season at U.C.L.A. Lew proved that he was not only big but aggressive on the boards. Here he drives for the basket as the rival Georgia Tech players look on, helpless to stop him.   *United Press International Photo*

except a six-man zone. Notre Dame tried a four-man zone, with one guard permanently assigned to Lew, and lost 96–67. The most common strategy was "freezing" the ball, or stalling it by dribbling and passing the ball back and forth in the backcourt so as to keep the ball out of action and give Lew as little chance to shoot, and score, as possible. Rival teams also tried to make Lew foul out by forcing him to remain too long under the basket on offense and by causing him to be called for goal-tending on defense. But for the most part these attempts to force Lew into fouling out failed (he only fouled out once that season), although he suffered many bruises from the grabbing, elbowing, and kicking of members of rival teams.

U.C.L.A. won all twenty-six games of that season to become one of the six major college teams ever to go unbeaten in regular season play. Lew's averages were twenty-nine and a half points and fifteen and a half rebounds per game. The season had not been much of a challenge to him, but Lew was exhilarated at the triumph, and at the post-game rally after U.C.L.A. had beaten Southern California 83–55 in the last game of the season, Lew took the microphone and yelled, "Keep the faith, baby!" The slogan, which the black congressman Adam Clayton Powell, Jr., always used, was for Lew an expression of black pride, but it was soon adopted by the U.C.L.A. fans to describe Lew's playing and to cheer him on.

Although the regular season had not been much of a

challenge to Lew, the NCAA championship tournament would be, for he and the U.C.L.A. team would
meet the University of Houston and its superstar, 6'8"
Elvin Hayes. Hayes was another much-talked-about
player, and the press was full of stories of a personal
rivalry between him and Alcindor. As far as Lew was
concerned, those stories were not true. He thought
Elvin Hayes was a fine player and looked forward to
playing against him, but he did not want to outplay
Elvin just to show he was better. He wanted to win
for his team, not to outdo Hayes. After easily beating
the University of Wyoming at Corvallis, Oregon,
U.C.L.A. traveled to Louisville, Kentucky, to meet the
University of Houston in what was billed as *the* game
of the year.

Early in the game it became clear that Houston's
strategy was to stay so close to Lew that he would
be forced to foul out. But Lew refused to fall into
the trap and only committed one or two fouls in the
entire game. Realizing that their first strategy was not
working, Houston put Hayes right on Lew to "psych"
him. This was the moment everyone had waited for,
including Lew, for he knew that Hayes was famous for
his "psyching." "Watch this!" Hayes would say when
he got the ball, and every time he was close to Lew he
would tell him how Houston would show U.C.L.A.
how the game was played. Psyching was part of the
game, and Lew was not angry at Elvin, but the psyching did seem to affect his playing. In the end, Elvin

outscored and out-rebounded Lew, but U.C.L.A. won, 73–58.

Lew was not especially smug after the game. He was glad his team had won, but he did not try to psych Hayes back when the two met after the game. He was more interested in getting to know Hayes and he thought they parted good friends. But later, to sportswriters, Hayes criticized Lew's "wonder boy" image, saying he was not aggressive enough either on offense or defense and not nearly as good as he was reported to be. When he heard of Hayes's criticism Lew was angry, but knowing anger would interfere with his concentration on the next tournament game, he put it out of his mind.

In the final game of the tournament, U.C.L.A. played the University of Dayton. Dayton used a 2–3 zone defense to stop Lew and held him to only twenty points. But like other teams before it, Dayton paid too much attention to Lew, and Mike Warren, Lucius Allen, and Lynn Shackleford were left free to score. Meanwhile Lew continued to control the backboards, blocking shot after shot and almost singlehandedly destroying Dayton's defense. The U.C.L.A. Bruins came from behind to win the game 79–64 and became the fourth team in NCAA history to go through a whole season and the championship playoffs without losing a single game.

Now honors and praise came rushing in from all sides. Lew was named to every major All-American team and chosen player of the year by a United Press International poll. There were reports that the Harlem Globetrotters, who had persuaded Wilt Chamberlain to leave Kansas University after his junior year in exchange for about fifty thousand dollars, had offered Lew a lifetime contract for one million dollars. But to all reporters' questions about this rumor, Lew answered that he wanted to get his education before he turned to considering any offers.

By that time Lew had become self-possessed enough to stop and talk to reporters occasionally, although he rarely sat down for an interview. But the reporters still resented his silence of the previous year and his criticism of U.C.L.A. and Californians. While praising his skill as a basketball player, they continued to describe him as a sullen young man who kept to himself. After a while it seemed to Lew that no matter what he said, it was twisted to fit his negative image. That hurt him. He was particularly hurt by an incident that occurred with a reporter to whom he actually talked for fifteen or twenty minutes. The reporter seemed interested in Lew not just as a basketball player but as a person, and Lew found himself telling the man about reading the *Autobiography of Malcolm X* and about his feeling that racial hatred, white and black, would destroy America if it was not cured. As Lew talked, the reporter jotted notes on his pad, and Lew thought they were notes about what he was saying. Whatever the notes were, the article that later appeared said that Lew was eccentric and surly and that he should be given a one-way ticket back to New York City. Right then and there, Lew realized it was useless to trust white reporters.

Pretty soon, Lew and fellow teammate Lucius Allen, who had also been experiencing a lot of prejudice and unhappiness at U.C.L.A., began to spend much of their time talking about all the other schools they could have gone to and wishing that they had chosen *any* of them over U.C.L.A. Lew particularly regretted not having gone to the University of Michigan, and wished that he had not been so blinded by his vision of California. In fact, one night both Lew and Lucius made up their minds to transfer—Lew to Michigan and Lucius to the University of Kansas. They knew that by transferring they would lose a season of basketball, but that night they were so fed up with U.C.L.A. that they just did not care. Of course they never went through with those decisions, for neither wanted to lose that year of basketball. Instead, they decided to think of U.C.L.A. as a job, something to perform acceptably and to forget about at the end of the day. Neither knew at that time that one of them would not be able to live up to that decision.

For the remainder of the school term, Lew again delved into his studies of Islam and the history of the black race, and thus he was able to get through the last months of his sophomore year. At last, as he said later, "When the school year was over, I put on an African robe and got into my car and headed home. I was shaking with excitement when I saw the New

York skyline. I thought I'd never make it to the house. Then I walked inside, sat down on the sofa and, for some reason, I started to cry. I still don't know over what."

That summer was one of the happiest of Lew's life, for he worked with boys in the ghetto areas of New York City. He and Emmette Bryant and Eddie Crawford, both members of the New York Knicks, were paid by Operation Sports Rescue of the New York City Housing Authority to travel around to the various ghetto areas and talk to the kids about basketball and show them some shots and moves. The youngsters' excitement at seeing him reminded Lew of his own early hero-worship of basketball stars, especially Wilt Chamberlain. "I used to shoot like him, comb my hair like him, the whole bit. Now kids in the ghetto are doing the same thing with me. I worry about the kids in the ghetto. I've got to get myself ready. I want to improve conditions for our people."

After that summer Lew was again in better spirits, and he returned to U.C.L.A. without the feeling of dread that had become so familiar. But his mood was soon to change, for he would become involved in a controversy that would bring more criticism upon him than he had ever experienced before.

By the fall of 1967 the country was beginning to talk about which American athletes would compete in the 1968 Olympic Games. At the same time, many black people in the country were remembering the black athletes who had competed in the previous Olympic

Games, won many medals, and afterward been subjected to the same discrimination as ever. Some felt deeply that such injustice should be protested and that black athletes should demonstrate their anger against such treatment of black athletes by boycotting the Olympics. On Thanksgiving Day 1967, some two hundred black athletes met in Los Angeles to discuss the possibility of a boycott. Among them were Mike Warren and Lew Alcindor.

Lew attended the meeting only after giving the matter a great deal of thought. He was not one to get involved in such a controversial issue on the spur of the moment. He realized the press would criticize him more than ever if he joined this cause, and that his career both at U.C.L.A. and afterward might be jeopardized. But he kept thinking of Cassius Clay (Muhammad Ali) walking into a restaurant with his Olympic gold medal around his neck and not being served, and he decided that he would be betraying black Americans if he did not join the cause.

Nevertheless, after the meeting (at which no definite decision to boycott had been made) Lew felt it was very important to explain his reason for attending the meeting and considering taking part in the boycott. Against his better judgment, he consented to one of his rare interviews.

He should have known he would not be given a chance to express things the way he wanted to. The reporters pressed him to say whether or not there would be a boycott, and when he would not give a definite answer they asked him how he personally felt about the boycott, how he would solve the racial problems in the United States, and other questions that Lew could not explain or give a definite answer to. He had hoped to be able to explain his conflicts—to let the public know that it was hard for him to be black and experience discrimination in America and resent America, and at the same time to care about America and want to shock it into becoming better. But the reporters would not let him just talk. They kept asking questions to which he could not give a positive answer, and when they could not get anything positive, they became angry and acted as if he were lying to them.

The resulting stories were very critical of Lew, and because of them he received a lot of hate mail. People called him ungrateful, said he should be barred from basketball and thrown out of U.C.L.A. Throughout the controversy, the U.C.L.A. athletic department and administration said nothing, put no pressure upon Lew, and he was grateful for that. No matter what he had said or done at U.C.L.A., as long as it had not interfered with his basketball playing or that of the rest of the team, no pressure had been brought upon him. Thus, although he had made many critical comments about U.C.L.A. and its students, he made it clear that he was not criticizing the athletic department.

Although Lew's part in the boycott controversy continued to be mentioned in the press from time to time, it was soon overshadowed by coverage of the U.C.L.A. team's basketball season, which showed promise of being as successful as the previous season. For the first part of the season, Lew and the rest of the team played well and won every game. Then, eight days before the Bruins were to play against Houston, Lew suffered a scratched eyeball in a game. To a basketball player, whose game depends so much upon clear vision and depth perception, an eye injury is very serious. Lew had to stay in bed in a dark room with a patch over his eye for three days, and even after that he was unable to practice with the rest of the team. He had to miss games against Portland and Stanford, and it was rumored that he would be unable to play against Houston. But Lew was determined not to miss that game. He believed that the team needed him and would not be able to win without him. He thought that he would be able to help the team even though his eye was not completely healed and even though, for the first time since he had begun to play basketball in elementary school, he was out of shape.

Lew soon found out that he was wrong. When the game began he felt just as he had when he had played his first game on a full court. The court seemed as long as a football field, and within five minutes he was exhausted, but he kept on, unable to believe that he could not play well if he really tried. But he could not play well, and this time Elvin Hayes's psyching had little to do with it. Lew made only four baskets out of eighteen tries—the first time he had ever shot less than fifty percent. His teammates, too, did not play well. No matter how good they were, Lew was still the center of their strategy and their game. Lew knew it, and even though he was not playing well he remained in the game, hoping he and his teammates could get it back together.

Even with U.C.L.A. playing poorly, Houston only beat the Bruins by two points, 71–69, but the loss ended U.C.L.A.'s forty-seven-game winning streak, and the Bruins were crushed. Lew was dejected; he blamed himself for being so determined to play and for not asking to be replaced after the first five minutes. In the locker room he shook his fist and vowed, "Never again, never again."

The press, of course, was full of the news of U.C.L.A.'s loss to Houston and Lew's loss to Elvin Hayes. On the basis of that one game, the Associated Press and United Press International polls showed Houston the number one college team and U.C.L.A. second. That angered the Bruins, and they determined to win back their number one spot when they next played Houston. They did not discuss revenge, but each player acquired a quiet determination that stayed with him throughout the rest of the season. The only thing Lew did openly to express his determination was to cut out and paste on his locker a cover of *Sports Illustrated* that showed Hayes shooting a basket over his head.

Lew's eye healed and soon he was back in his old form. The rest of the U.C.L.A. team also quickly perked up after the game with Houston. Coach Wooden came up with a new "trap zone" strategy that enabled U.C.L.A.'s wing men to take off more quickly after Lew cleared the boards; and the rest of the team now had a chance to play more because Edgar Lacey had quit. The happiness of most of the players who were able to play more was dampened, however, by their knowledge of why Lacey had ended his U.C.L.A. basketball career.

The end of Lacey's career had begun at the Houston game. He had been one of the five starters, assigned to guard Elvin Hayes, but when Hayes had scored twenty-nine points before the first half was over, Wooden had taken Lacey out. Several other U.C.L.A. players, including Lew, were tried against Hayes, and only toward the end of the game were the Bruins able to slow him down. Lacey greatly resented having to sit out the entire second half of such an important game, and after the game he told Lew that he was going to quit. Of course Lew did not want Lacey to quit but he understood his friend's humiliation. He also felt somewhat guilty because Wooden had sent Lacey to the bench while he had allowed Lew to stumble around out of shape and with a bad eye for the entire game. Lew and Lacey had their own opinion of why Wooden had made the choices he had. That opinion was based on Wooden's character and his attitudes toward his players and their habits.

Wooden had a reputation for being one of the most morally strict college coaches. He did not smoke, drink, or swear. He would not allow any card games except cribbage to be played on the bus on road trips, and any player who swore on the court during practice or a game was benched. He even frowned upon practical jokes among the players. Wooden expected his players to have the same attitudes as he did, and any player who behaved "improperly" was considered not "morally" ready for play. Edgar Lacey did not have the same attitudes as Wooden and he refused to conform to them. As a result, he found himself fighting for a starting position that he felt should have been his automatically.

This attitude of Wooden's had long bothered Lacey, and the Houston game had been the last straw. He—and Lew—hoped Wooden would say something to appease him in the next week, but although Wooden made general remarks that everyone on the team knew were meant especially for Lacey, he did not speak directly to Lacey or mention him by name. That was too much for the sensitive Lacey, and he never played for U.C.L.A. again.

The press carried rumors that Lew had had something to do with Lacey's quitting, and that hurt Lew. He was very close to Lacey; together they had gotten through some bad periods for both of them at U.C.L.A. Lew knew Lacey did not believe the rumors; he just hoped none of their friends did either.

U.C.L.A. finished its regular season having lost only the one game to Houston, and thus was eligible for the West Regional playoffs in Albuquerque, New Mexico. In the University of New Mexico Arena the Bruins played New Mexico State and the University of New Mexico on successive nights and captured the West Regional title. Houston meanwhile had also qualified for the NCAA championship playoffs, and the moment for which both teams, especially U.C.L.A., had been waiting since the game in January was at hand.

The big game was played at U.C.L.A. The week before, U.C.L.A. had worked out a new arrangement which was called a "diamond and one." Lew was sure it would be successful. Mike Warren would be out on the point and Mike Lynn and Lucius Allen would be at the sides of the foul line on the corners of the diamond. Lew, under the basket, would make the fourth point. Lynn Shackleford would be the "one" of the "diamond and one," his job being to guard Elvin Hayes. The formation would take a lot of concentration.

The game had hardly started when Elvin Hayes came up to Lew and boasted, "Man, we're gonna beat you! We're gonna beat you bad!" Every time he got close to Lew he would launch into a stream of banter, but Lew hardly heard him. He was too busy playing just as well as he could.

Lew played a fine game, as did the other U.C.L.A. players, especially Lynn Shackleford who guarded Hayes so well that the Houston star made only five points in the first half and five in the second. U.C.L.A. won heartily, 101–69, and the team insists that the margin could have been greater except that by the second half there was no more challenge to play well.

Hayes disappeared after the game and could not be found for comment.

Oh, revenge was sweet! Lew had brought a brightly colored striped African robe to the game in his gym bag, knowing that Wooden would have been angry if he had worn it to the game. But after the game, "I didn't care what anybody thought. I had always wanted to show my pride in things black, and in the general exhilaration of beating Houston, I just hauled out the robe and put it on and walked right out of the locker room as big as life. Coach Wooden saw me, and all he did was smile. My mother saw me, and she said, 'My God!' and my father gave me a funny look. But after I explained to them why I was wearing the robe, my mother said, 'O.K., that's cool,' and my dad said he understood. They both knew I had my own way to go. Some people thought I was just trying to be a hot dog, to show off in the robe, but it wasn't that way at all. It was my way of saying I'm black and I'm proud of being black and here it is, man, you can take it or leave it. This is me." Lew had good reason to be proud. He had led his team to another NCAA championship and for the second year in a row was named Most Valuable Player of the NCAA Championship.

Lew's glory was not to last long. It was soon overshadowed by the bad publicity he now began to receive as a result of his decision to boycott the 1968 Olympics. He had given the matter much thought and finally he decided, along with a number of other black athletes, that it was time for him to stand up as a man and refuse to be used as a performing animal. Lew avoided the reporters as much as possible, and while other athletes were forming an Olympic basketball team Lew went back to New York City and Operation Sports Rescue. For him, talking to little ghetto children, urging them to stay in school so they might have a chance to make a future for themselves, was much more important than winning a gold medal in the Olympics.

But Lew's participation in the boycott was not to be forgotten. During that summer he was asked to make a guest appearance on the "Today Show" on NBC-TV in order, he thought, to publicize Operation Sports Rescue. But on the air he was asked why he was boycotting the Olympics, why he did not compete for his country. Lew answered that even though he lived in America it wasn't really his country. One of the program's moderators then suggested he ought to leave and Lew, really angry by this time, said that would be fine with him.

At that point a station break interrupted the program, and by the time the program resumed, Lew's time was up and he left. Another moderator told viewers that Lew had explained his last statement further to them off the air, but the damage had already been done. In an attempt to clear up the misunderstanding, Lew even invited reporters to his parents' home in Hollis, Queens, where they had recently moved. He knew that such occurrences could severely damage an athlete's image and career. He explained he really did not know what the moderator had meant when he had suggested that Lew move. Where did the man expect him to go, Lew asked—to Africa? What he was trying to get across, Lew explained, was that until black people were given equal treatment in America it was not really their country. If there were a country like America that did give equal treatment to blacks, then blacks should move to it. But no such country existed, and so black people preferred to change America rather than leave it.

Lew was able to ease the furor created as a result of the television program, but the incident continued to bother him. He was so tired of racism and of being drawn into racial arguments. He had long been look-ing for some way to escape the hatred and bitterness of the racial situation in America, and the more he read about the religion of Islam the more he turned to it for solace. There was no room for racial hatred in Islam, and Lew had come to realize that that was the way he felt in his heart. That summer he decided to convert to the religion of Islam.

In his readings Lew had found that the two largest groups in the religion of Islam were the Sunnites and the Shi'ites. The differences in religious practices of the two groups were few. Malcolm X had been a Sunnite, and partly because of admiration for the late black leader, Lew chose to become a Sunnite. He went to a Muslim mosque in Harlem to find out how to pre-pare for this, and there he met men of the Sunnite Muslims who agreed to instruct him. For the next few weeks, Lew got up at 6 A.M. every day to receive instruction from these teachers, who told him that if he did not want to get up early he did not want to become a Muslim. Lew learned the various religious rites and practices of the Muslim religion as well as its ethical beliefs, the most important of which is the belief that a Muslim is not judged by what he says or by how often he goes to the temple but by his acts.

Shortly before he was to return to U.C.L.A., Lew had his *shahada*, which is like a baptism, into the religion of Islam, and he received a new name, Kareem Abdul-Jabbar. Kareem means "noble and generous"; Abdul means "servant"; and Jabbar means "powerful." Together, they meant "the noble and generous servant of The Powerful [Allah, the Muslim God]." It was a religious name, and Lew was very proud of it; but he did not mind if his friends slipped and called him "Lew." In fact, he did not tell many people what he had done; his conversion was important to him but it was personal and he did not feel the need to proclaim it. Only his family and his close friends knew of the change at the time. Later, he would make the change public and sports reporters would refer to him by his Muslim name.

The members of the U.C.L.A. team who were not his close friends learned about Lew's conversion on the bus on the way to their third game of Lew's last U.C.L.A. season. He and Steve Paterson, a Protestant, began a discussion of religion that soon became very heated. They were joined by Donny Saffer, a Jew, and

Lew seems alone with the ball and the basket as he scores two points against Purdue in the first game of his senior year basketball season at U.C.L.A. All the Purdue players can do is wait for the rebound.   *United Press International Photo*

Terry Schofield, a Catholic. Coach Wooden also moved closer to listen. Eventually Lew stated that he had become a Muslim. For a moment everyone was silent, but soon the discussion was resumed and the topic became the Muslim religion. The others were genuinely interested in Lew's feelings and his reasons for converting to Islam. Coach Wooden seemed to accept it as well as everyone else. At the end of the bus ride, the whole team felt closer to one another and more willing to accept differences in each other. For Lew, that was one of the two most important things that happened during his last basketball season at U.C.L.A. Neither of them had anything to do with winning or losing.

The other important incident was the change in Coach Wooden's attitude about his players' "moral readiness" to play. The team had been reminded of Wooden's attitude again that year in the cases of Lucius Allen and Mike Lynn, neither of whom would be playing with the team that season.

Lucius Allen had gotten into trouble over possession of marijuana and had been suspended from the team. Lew felt very badly about that. He knew that Lucius had been troubled and unhappy, and he believed that if Coach Wooden had tried to understand Lucius' feelings, perhaps Lucius would never have felt the need for drugs. But Lew knew that Lucius' troubles went beyond basketball. He and Lucius had talked about leaving the team, but neither could have predicted that one of them would leave in this way.

Mike Lynn had gotten into trouble over a stolen credit card. He had been arrested, tried, and punished by the courts, but Wooden and the U.C.L.A. athletic department had further punished him by suspending him from the team for his senior year. Lynn did not think this action was fair, and Lew and some of the other members of the team agreed with him.

After Mike got into trouble, he became very friendly with Lew and his friends. "Until then, Mike had had the typical white-American attitude," Lew explains. "He didn't run around calling people nigger or anything like that, but you could see that he definitely thought in a stereotyped manner. . . . Now he knew what it was like to be barred from the Establishment, just like a black athlete; overnight he had become a minority race, and so he kind of drifted toward our little black group, and we got to know him well. He turned out to be a real man. He learned fast, and he lost his prejudices almost overnight. Mike Lynn is a great object lesson in how fast a white man can see the truth, provided he will listen."

Still, Lew was sorry Mike had to learn in such a hard way. As in Edgar Lacey's case, Mike Lynn's being off the team seemed to Lew to be a direct result of Coach Wooden's attitude toward his players' morality. Other players felt the same way, and a noticeable tension developed within the team.

Toward the end of the season, at a game against Drake University, the tension broke. With one minute left in the game, Wooden told a player named Bill

Sweek to get ready to go onto the floor. Sweek, who did not usually get to play very often, eagerly stood up, but a few seconds later Wooden motioned him to sit down again. Angrily, Sweek headed for the locker room. Players were not supposed to leave the floor until the game was over, but Sweek did not care. He was tired of Wooden's attitude. Maybe he was not one of the best players, but he felt he could have played more if he had fit Wooden's ideal. When Wooden confronted Sweek in the shower room the angry player said exactly what he thought—that not everyone had to belong to the Fellowship of Christian Athletes or be a grind at his studies or think exactly the way Wooden did in order to be a good player. "Maybe," he said to Wooden, "some of the trouble is with you."

The rest of the team witnessed the argument and wondered what Wooden would do. Many were glad Sweek had spoken out, for they had often wanted to do so themselves. At the same time, they liked Wooden; he was a fine coach and, despite his rigid attitudes, a good man. It was a tense time for the entire U.C.L.A. team.

The next day, just before practice, Wooden called the team together. Quietly and seriously he made the team understand that he had thought about what Sweek had said and that he had learned something. He was going to try harder to understand players like Bill Sweek, who was not going to be put off the team. Sweek apologized for walking off the floor, and the two shook hands. From the rest of the team came an almost audible sigh of relief and their faces showed a new respect for their coach. They knew how hard it must have been for him to admit he might have been wrong. It was these incidents of the basketball season of his senior year—where people came to a greater understanding and closeness with each other—that Lew would remember best, not winning and losing games.

U.C.L.A.'s regular season play was little different from that of previous seasons. The University of Southern California used a stall strategy in one game and edged out by two points a U.C.L.A. team that just could not get going. But U.C.L.A. won all its other games, and for the fourth year in a row went on to the NCAA championship tournament.

On the Sunday before the final game of that tournament, Lew opened a copy of *West* Magazine, a supplement of the *Los Angeles Times,* and was shocked to find a very damaging article about himself. Written by a former official of the Black Students Union, an organization of black students at U.C.L.A., it portrayed Lew as a hate-filled black separatist, dissatisfied with his school and his country, wanting no part of white America. Lew was very upset about the article. Of course he had made some critical statements about white America—what black man hadn't? —but he had also made many attempts to explain those statements so they would not appear too harsh. What he found almost more upsetting was the language and grammar of some of the statements that the article quoted him as having made. He had a high IQ, 131, but these statements made him sound foolish and illiterate!

The next evening Lew called his teammates together to explain his side. He also arranged to appear on a Los Angeles television program to refute most of what had been written in the article. He was not going to allow that article to go unanswered.

Coach Wooden sympathized with Lew, but he had called for strict silence on the part of the members of the team until the tournament was over, and he did not feel he could allow Lew to break that silence. At practice the next day, he advised Lew to cancel the television appearance. Lew angrily walked out of the practice.

Until that day, despite his feelings about Edgar Lacey, Mike Lynn, and the others who had clashed with Wooden, Lew had not had a personal gripe against his coach. Wooden had kept his strict attitudes to himself when Lew had criticized U.C.L.A. and Californians and during the Olympic boycott controversy. While Lew realized there could have been an ulterior motive behind Wooden's silence—after all, Lew was too valuable a player to antagonize—the fact remained that Wooden had given him a pretty free rein. But how could Wooden expect him to keep silent about the article, Lew wondered. He *had* to get himself straight with people.

In the end, Lew did appear on the television program. Coach Wooden had realized how deeply upset

Lew was and how important it was for him to make that appearance. If he had been forced to remain silent, he would have been unable to play well in the tournament game. All week the players had been tense and Lew, for one, had been fighting against a strange and unexplainable fear of losing. The magazine article and the possibility of not being able to answer its charges had brought him almost to the breaking point. But after the television program, much of the tension ebbed away, and what remained was the tension a player needs if he is to be ready for a game—the taut expectancy of a sprinter crouched and ready for the starting gun to go off. Lew and his team played a fine game against Purdue University and won its third straight NCAA championship. Lew was named Most Valuable Player in the NCAA championship for the third time in a row and became the first—and perhaps the last—player to win the honor three times.

Now it was time for celebration, but Lew did not join in wholeheartedly. He was worried about Lucius Allen. He had expected Lucius to be at the game, but he had not seen him, and he thought it strange, for Lucius had visited Lew only the day before. Lew had received a watch for being Most Valuable Player and he wanted to give it to his friend.

Even after the team had piled into a bus and cars to go to an out-of-town team dinner, Lew kept looking for Lucius. Someone telephoned the place where Lucius was staying and spoke to him, but no one

Basketball observers marvel at how such a big man can be so graceful. Here, in the first half of the NCAA Western Regional Basketball championship in his senior year at U.C.L.A., Lew's movements seem effortless as he scores two more points against Santa Clara. U.C.L.A. won the game 90–52.

United Press International Photo

knew when he was coming. He never arrived, and thus the happiness of the post-game celebration was, for Lew, tinged with sadness.

Lew's entire U.C.L.A. basketball career had been a mixture of happiness and sadness, good and bad. His influence upon the team's playing had been so strong—if he was playing poorly, the rest of the team usually played poorly too—that he had often borne the chief responsibility for whatever happened on or off the court. Wrongly, he had been under suspicion when Edgar Lacey had quit the team, when Mike Lynn had gotten into trouble over the stolen credit card, and when Lucius Allen had been charged with possession of marijuana. Although anyone who knew Lew knew he had had nothing to do with those incidents, many members of the press had preferred to believe otherwise. A story about Lew Alcindor that hinted of scandal had always been better copy than one that did not. Lew had borne much more than his share of the pressure during his U.C.L.A. basketball career.

Now that career was over, but Lew faced a new pressure—that of deciding which professional basketball team to sign with. (Lew exceeded military height limitations so did not have to worry about being drafted into the army.) As long as he had been eligible to play for U.C.L.A. the professional teams were not allowed to talk with him, although some of them had tried to bypass the rule, but now that Lew was available recruiters and offers came in droves, from both the National Basketball Association (NBA) and the

American Basketball Association (ABA). Lew listened to all the offers, but he already had a preference—he wanted to play with the New York Nets. All his life he had wanted to play with the New York Knicks, an NBA team, but the Knicks had not won the right to draft him. So he decided he would be almost as happy with the Nets, an ABA team. At least he would be able to play for his home town.

Two U.C.L.A. alumni volunteered to help Lew in his negotiations with the two professional leagues, and he gratefully accepted their help. Late in March, the three traveled to New York to begin the official negotiations. They first met with the commissioner of the NBA and with the owner of the Milwaukee Bucks, the NBA team that had won the right to draft Lew. The Bucks made a five-year offer for 1.4 million dollars. Lew liked the offer but wanted to wait until he heard what the ABA and the Nets would offer the next day. He was disappointed when the ABA and the Nets offered considerably less money. Lew and his advisers had decided before going to New York that they would not get involved in a long, drawn-out bidding situation, and thus, although he would have preferred to play with the Nets, Lew accepted the Bucks' offer. That evening the ABA asked Lew to wait one more day, for the league would make another offer. Lew wanted to wait, but he had given his word to the NBA, and after talking the situation over with his father he decided not to break his promise. Lew was unhappy about the outcome of the negotiations at the time, but he was glad he had kept his word, and later he would be glad he had gone to the more stable and older NBA league.

With his future decided for the next five years at least, Lew returned to U.C.L.A. and settled back to finish his senior year, particularly to writing his senior thesis, which he wrote on Islam in North America. At graduation, in his cap and gown, he stood head and shoulders above nearly everyone else and received his Bachelor of Arts degree in history and recognition for having maintained a B— average. Then, as soon as he could, he packed up his belongings and headed home to New York. It had been a strange four years; no matter what the future held, he thought, it would have to be better.

4
To Win Some and Lose Some

LEW LOOKED FORWARD WITH GREAT EXCITEMENT TO playing with the professionals. Sometimes he would lie awake at night and try to picture himself playing with the Bucks against other professional teams. He was really looking forward to winning some and losing some and learning all the time. In contrast to his careers at Power Memorial and U.C.L.A., no one was going to expect the Bucks to win every game, and it would be much more fun. Never again would he have to bear the pressure that he bore as a publicized schoolboy athlete. He would not have to worry about his studies, and he would not have to worry as much about his relationships with his teammates and his coaches. He was a man and he would be treated as a man.

Professional basketball, with all its excitement and pressure, is a job, and the relationship between coaches and their players is more businesslike than it is in school basketball. Lew had always cared deeply how his coaches felt about him and his fellow teammates. This involvement had often been the basis for much of the pressure he had felt. Coach Jack Donohue had tried to be a father to him and had been so authoritarian that Lew had felt caged. Coach John Wooden had not been authoritarian, but his strict moral attitudes had caused Lew to feel uncomfortable. Lew had not gotten to know Larry Costello yet, but he realized that his relationship with the Bucks' coach would never reach the personal level that had characterized his relationships with Donohue and Wooden. The names the three coaches chose to call him revealed the differences in his relationships with them: while Donohue had called him "Lewie" and Wooden had called him "Lewis," Costello just called him "Lew."

Because he was, finally, free from the kinds of pressure he had endured ever since he became famous at Power Memorial, Lew was now able to break his long silence and to tell the public, in his own words, who Lew Alcindor really was and how he really felt about his school athletic career. A writer for *Sports Illustrated* had suggested that Lew tell his story for serialization in that magazine, and Lew agreed. "My Story" was the first complete chronicle of Lew's life and the first complete expression of Lew's feelings about his life. Until then, the public had read only other people's opinions of him or short quotations of his remarks.

In Atlanta, Georgia, at the end of his final season at U.C.L.A., Lew, who had led his team to an unprecedented third straight NCAA championship, was awarded the first James A. Naismith Award as the nation's top college basketball player.

United Press International Photo

Lew had found many of these opinions unfair and many of his remarks misquoted, but except in extreme cases he had not publicly responded to them or told his own side. Now he did. But Lew did not tell his story simply because he wanted to answer all those who had written or talked about him or because he was conceited. In the beginning of "My Story" he said: "The way things are in America today—and have been for 200 years—the story of any black man has meaning, even if he's a shoeshine 'boy' or a porter or your friendly neighborhood Uncle Tom. Maybe you won't read about them; maybe you will read about me because you are interested in basketball. That's fine. A long time ago I learned to accept the idea that people have no interest in me except as a jock. But I'm also a person, a human being, just like those other black men who walk about invisible to many of their fellows."

Ever since he had begun to feel pride in his own race, Lew had not been content simply to be "a jock." His fame had been a burden at times, but it had also given him an opportunity to speak out as a black man in white America, and he had taken advantage of that opportunity whenever he could. Thus he continued the tradition of Bill Russell, Muhammad Ali, and Jim Brown, all of whom established themselves as sports superstars and then revealed how deeply they resented the role of the black man in American society. They had proved themselves forces to be reckoned with, not only as professional athletes but as spokesmen for their race. Now Lew was entering their ranks.

The press was full of speculation about how Lew would fare in pro basketball, and the controversy and air of expectancy were to mount until the opening of the Milwaukee season. Lew had always felt that it was silly to worry about the future, and so after graduation he went back to New York to spend a quiet vacation with his family. With some of the money he had received for signing with the Bucks he bought a new wardrobe, a Cadillac so he would at last have a car in which he did not feel cramped, and a set of drums. After his vacation, he moved out to Milwaukee and began preparing in earnest for pro basketball, getting to know his teammates and learning how to play with them in the tough, driving pro game.

Lew's first professional appearance came before the regular league season, in an exhibition game against the Phoenix Suns in Milwaukee Arena. The game was only moments old when he scored a three-point play that many observers took to be an omen for his professional career. The rest of his offensive play was much the same. Once he took a pass at the free-throw line and, from there, stuffed it!

The Suns had not expected to stop Lew on offense, but they soon found that he made a change even in their defensive strategy necessary. Gone were the drives down under the basket for easy shots—Lew was always there to block them. Once, toward the end of the fourth period, he blocked a shot from ten feet away from the basket, and then popped up under the basket to block the follow-up shot. His speed and agility amazed observers most; they marveled at how such a big man could move so quickly. But anyone who really knew Lew was not surprised. His speed and agility were the result of long years of training, beginning with hours of track practice at St. Jude's. In the Bucks' pre-season running trials, Lew had run the 300-yard race faster than anyone else on the team —in 38.9 seconds.

But Lew was still a rookie and he still had a lot to learn. Early in the season he found that he would have to polish his strategy of blocking shots if he did not want to be called for goal tending. For a while the officials called goal tending nearly every time he blocked a shot, and in reaction to these calls Lew stopped trying to block shots and simply got the rebound after his opponent shot. Only gradually did he begin to block shots again, realizing that the risk of being called for goal tending was preferable to the fear of taking that risk.

That season Lew also experienced more than once the feeling of having scored less than other members of his team, such as Flynn Robinson and Jon McGlocklin, *and* the feeling of losing. But while he was failing to be high scorer in every game, he was steadily developing into a fine defensive player; and while his team was not winning every game, he was gaining experience playing against some of the top professional basketball players in the country. By the end of the regular NBA season all observers were full of praise for Lew and the way he had developed. He had quickly graduated from rookie to full professional status, and he was credited with almost singlehandedly carrying the Bucks from a poor last place in the NBA Eastern Division to second place and eligible for the division playoffs. In April 1970 the young, inexperienced Bucks began the playoff series against the powerful New York Knicks.

From the beginning the tournament was a mismatch. The Knicks were an experienced team, used to playing with each other, aware of what each player could do. They were a strong and talented team—the backcourt men could shoot baskets from twenty feet away with amazing accuracy and the Knicks substitutes would have made a formidable team in themselves. By contrast, the Bucks were young and inexperienced in playing with each other; they relied so heavily upon Lew that an off-night for him or a good defensive strategy against him almost inevitably meant a loss for his team.

The Knicks won the first two games, using a strategy of ganging up on Lew defensively and having supershooter Willis Reed match him in individual high scoring. In the first game the Knicks substitutes scored 24 points, while the Bucks substitutes scored none. The Milwaukee guards not only had difficulty protecting the ball, they were unable to get it inside to Lew with any consistency. When Lew did have the ball, the Knicks double-teamed him, occasionally stealing the ball and often forcing him to take poor shots. But despite the fine, strong playing of the Knicks, the Bucks won the third game of the series 101–96, mostly on the basis of Lew's performance—the best performance of his professional career, in the opinion of many. The rest of the team played poorly.

The next game, Lew was off defensively. Although he scored thirty-eight points and led his teammates from twenty points behind, the Knicks won. The fifth game was played at Madison Square Garden in New York and the Knicks gave a dazzling performance to trounce the Bucks 132–96 and win the Eastern Division playoffs.

Lew was disappointed at having lost the playoffs, but he realized that it would have been a miracle if his team had beaten the Knicks. The Bucks had a lot to learn—and so did he. There would be many more seasons and more tournaments; maybe the Bucks would win some of those tournaments. He was pleased to hear that the Knicks players had praised his playing and that they had been embarrassed by the New York fans' reaction when it became clear that the Knicks had won.

That really rankled—the reaction of his "home town" fans. As the final game slipped out of the Bucks' reach and Lew was taken out of the game, the crowd had begun to chant, "Good-bye, Lewie, we hate to see you go." It was strange—Lew had been such a hero in New York for so many years. "I used to like to play in New York," Lew said later. "Now I don't have any feelings, or perhaps I should say I don't like it.

There are a lot of nasty, small people here. It's gotten so I have to play Goliath every time I'm here."

All his life, New York had been home for Lew. Especially while he was at U.C.L.A. it had been a kind of haven for him—a place where he could escape the unhappiness he experienced in California. Now he felt alienated from New York, in a way, or at least from people like those who had sat in Madison Square Garden and booed him. But his parents were still there, and Harlem; there was a black culture in New York, and black people who cared about him as a person, not as "a jock." And no matter how much the fans booed, New York was better than Milwaukee.

Even though he had an apartment in Milwaukee, Lew didn't really feel that he lived there. He existed there, perhaps, but he didn't really *live* there.

Compared to Milwaukee, New York and even California were paradise. At least he had roots there. "In New York or on the West Coast there is a black culture. That is why I get to New York as often as I can during the season and why I bought a house in central Los Angeles. Here, I'm this strange object. I go out to the dry cleaners or a record shop or maybe for groceries, and they gawk and point. I can't go to the regular movies so I tried a drive-in but got wasted by the cold the second time."

Even with the team, when they were not playing, Lew kept to himself. On bus rides to games in other cities he would throw his coat over his head and beneath it he would sleep or listen to music on the tape recorder that was his constant traveling companion. His teammates were good people, but off the court he didn't have much in common with them.

It was as much a lift for Lew as for the Bucks when shortly after losing the tournament to the Knicks, the Bucks traded with the Cincinnati Royals for Oscar Robertson. Robertson, 6'5", had ten years of NBA experience, a lifetime scoring average of 29.3, a perfect 10-year All-Star selection record, and the unique status of being the best playmaker of all time. He was a prize for the Bucks and a bonus for Lew.

Lew remembered the first time he ever played with Oscar Robertson. It was at a summer resort just before Lew began to play professional basketball. Oscar had driven down the middle and Lew had gone right in behind him. Oscar turned around and yelled at Lew, telling him that if he had made a certain cut Oscar would have been wide open. So the next time Oscar drove, Lew cut his way, even though he didn't think Oscar was open at all. To Lew's surprise, suddenly the ball was in his hands. It was like magic.

Robertson was very critical and demanding when it came to basketball, but that was understandable. Never before in his professional career had he had the opportunity to play with a big man like Lew. Although he was acknowledged to be one of the best players in pro basketball history, he had never been on a championship team. It was terribly frustrating, and as the years had passed Robertson had become more and more anxious to win a championship, and more and more demanding of his teammates. Lew realized Oscar would be a hard taskmaster, but he was looking forward to it. Robertson would help balance a team that relied too heavily on Lew. He would take a great deal of pressure off Lew and allow him to concentrate more on his offensive strategy.

That summer the Bucks also traded with the Seattle Supersonics for 6'8" forward Bob Boozer, a player with experience and wisdom equal to Robertson's, and, Lew could hardly believe it, Lucius Allen!

Since graduating from U.C.L.A., Lew and Lucius had kept in touch, but it was hard to keep up a friendship when both were so busy with their basketball careers. Now they would be together again. It would be good for both to have someone around who had shared some of the same memories and feelings, and it would be good to play together again. Lucius understood the game and would give added speed on offense and defense. After playing with each other at U.C.L.A. for so long, it would be possible for the two to play easily together now.

Lew had never enjoyed preparing for a season as much as he did for the 1970–71 season. As the team continued to practice together, he could feel it becoming a real team, not just five basketball players. The Bucks got better and better, and by the first game of the regular season, against the Atlanta Hawks, all eyes were on the Bucks and the Alcindor–Robertson combination.

In that game, although Robertson scored only 15

points, he ran a deliberate game and set up plays to enable Lew to score 32 points and for Bob Dandridge to put in 21 more. Scoring 33 points in the final quarter, the Bucks came from behind to win 107–98. The rest of the season was much the same story. The Bucks seemed to treat every game like a demolition derby, outscoring their opponents by 13 points per game. Observers marveled at their energy. By February their record was 43–9 and they were nine games ahead in the Midwest Division.

Meanwhile, the New York Knicks' record was only 38–18, and yet the Bucks just could not seem to play their usual game against the Knicks. In the first two meetings between the teams, the Bucks had the games won until the last four or five minutes. Then they just seemed to stop playing! It was strange, unexplainable. Despite their otherwise outstanding records, the Bucks beat the Knicks only once in five games that season.

What a contest the NBA Championship Tournament would be if the Knicks and the Bucks were to play against each other in it! Even before the end of the regular season, basketball fans were talking about it. With the magic of the Alcindor-Robertson combination and their fine won-lost record, there was little doubt that the Bucks would reach the championship tournament. The Knicks' chance of reaching the tournament was more questionable. They had suffered many injuries during the year, and their record had shown it. But the Knicks had an ability that few other teams possessed to pull together and really get "up" for a game. With a chance to play the Bucks for the NBA crown as the prize, the Knicks would give their all to the regular season and playoff games.

When the regular season ended, the won-lost records of the two teams qualified them for the semifinals in their divisions, the Knicks to play the Atlanta Hawks in the Eastern Division and the Bucks to play the San Francisco Warriors in the Western Division. At the end of March 1971 the two semifinal playoff series began.

Milwaukee took its series easily from San Francisco, winning each of the first three games by at least 12 points, losing the fourth by a mere two points on a night when they were just "off," and roaring back to clobber San Francisco 136–86 and to win the tournament in five games. The Knicks, meanwhile, also won their series in five games, although their scoring margins were very small against Atlanta, a team that had not even won half its games in the regular season. The Knicks' play seemed surprisingly disorganized, but they were still in there, and some basketball fans began to make bets on either the Knicks or the Bucks for the NBA Championship.

But there was yet another playoff series in each division before the contenders for the championship tournament would be known for sure. Now the Bucks faced the Los Angeles Lakers for the Western Division Championship, and the Knicks were matched with the Baltimore Bullets in the Eastern Division. The Bucks

As a professional, Lew has the opportunity to play against some of his long-time heroes. Nate Thurmond of the San Francisco Warriors (42) is the player Lew most looked forward to playing against. Here Lew hooks a shot over Thurmond's head as the Bucks move toward their second victory in the 1971 NBA playoffs.   *United Press International Photo*

again won easily, taking the series in five games, and by at least 18 points in each of the four games they won.

Meanwhile the Knicks were having a tough time against the Baltimore Bullets. They won the first game by only one point, picked up momentum decidedly with a 107–88 win in the second game, but lost miserably in the third game, 114–88. They lost again in the fourth game, won by 5 points in the fifth game, and lost 113–96 in the sixth. Their injuries showed. Cazzie Russell had never recovered his touch after breaking his wrist, and Willis Reed was definitely slower. The pressing defense that had always before been their strength seemed gone, and the substitute team did not come through as it had in the past. Nevertheless, when it came to the seventh game both the Knicks and their fans were sure they would come through; they had had a lot of experience in tournaments and had been in many other tight situations.

The seventh game of that tournament was one of the tightest situations the Knicks had ever experienced. With only a few seconds left in the game the score was 93–91 in favor of Baltimore. Then the Knicks got the ball, and the cool Bill Bradley was given the chance to save his team. He took the shot—and missed. The Knicks' reign as champions of the NBA was over. A little luck and the Bucks might have faced the Knicks instead of the Bullets in the NBA Championship Tournament.

The Bucks were disappointed. They had wanted to

play the Knicks, to show that although the Knicks had outplayed them in the regular season games they could get their revenge in the tournament. But winning that NBA tournament was the most important thing, especially for Oscar Robertson. After over a decade in professional basketball Robertson finally had a chance to be on a championship team, and he, who usually set the mood for the entire Bucks team, made it known in no uncertain terms that he would not muff this chance.

On April 21, 1971, the NBA Championship series began. The Baltimore Bullets had been called a Cinderella team because of the great odds it had overcome to arrive at the series, but the Alcindor-Robertson combination proved too much for them. The Bucks won the first game, 98–88. In the second game they were even more impressive. Lew was at his most agile, making several plays that would have been remarkable even for a man a foot shorter, and Oscar called the plays as smoothly as ever. The Bullets kept up with the Bucks until the end of the first quarter, but after that they could not maintain their momentum. The Bucks won the third game, too, and now the championship was really in their grasp. When interviewed by reporters, Lew and Oscar did not seem excited. Lew spoke of the work and concentration involved in the series; Oscar said he had played too long to get excited. But the 10,746 Bucks fans at the game were very excited, and after the game, which was played in Milwaukee, they saluted Alcindor and

Robertson and their teammates as if the championship had already been won.

The fans were right. Led by Oscar Robertson, the Bucks trounced the Bullets 118–106 to win the series in four games and to become only the second team to do so in the NBA's twenty-five-year history. But although Robertson was given credit as the playmaker, Lew was the most important element in the win, and barely into his twenty-fourth year he was awarded basketball's biggest prize—Most Valuable Player of the NBA. For this he earned the sports car given each year by *Sports Magazine,* and it was comical to see him fold himself into the tiny car at the presentation ceremonies. But for Lew the true satisfaction was having won as a member of a real team, consisting of Oscar Robertson, Lucius Allen, Bob Boozer, and the others in addition to Lew Alcindor. This, to Lew, was what basketball was all about.

Barely a month later, Lew showed his fans that basketball was still not at the top of his list of priorities. On May 28, 1971, the first NBA-ABA All-Star game was held, but Lew was not in attendance. That evening he married Janice Brown, a schoolteacher, in Washington, D.C.

Nineteen seventy-one was to be a year full of momentous events for Lew, for in addition to winning his first NBA championship and getting married, he took a decisive step in his spiritual life. He had become convinced that Islam was the true faith for him and the one to which he wished to commit himself. When one commits oneself to the Islamic religion, one takes an Islamic name. Back in the summer of 1968, Lew had made a confession of faith and had been given such a name. He did not adopt it legally at that time because, as he later explained, "I wanted to make sure that my feelings were not a passing thing." By late summer of 1971 he knew they were not, and so he announced that he would change his name legally to Kareem Abdul-Jabbar and henceforth wished to be known by that name.

"Of course my parents were dead set against it," Kareem recalls. "The name change particularly hurt my father. I am his only child and a junior at that. Now there's no one to carry on his name." His parents thought he was ashamed of the name they had given him, and try as he might he could not seem to make them understand that his decision was not a negative step but a positive one. It was not that he disliked the name his parents had given him, but Kareem Abdul-Jabbar was for him a testimonial to his faith in Allah and Islam. His wife, too, changed her name, taking the Islamic name of Habiba.

Of course, Kareem was not the first major sports figure to adopt an Islamic name. Some years before, boxer Cassius Clay had become Muhammad Ali. Kareem could take some comfort in the knowledge that gradually the public had come to accept the heavyweight champion's new name and indeed had practically forgotten that his name had once been Clay. But there, in Kareem's eyes, the other man's function as a model ended. Muhammad Ali had joined the Black Muslims, who were not true Muslims in the view of traditional Islam. To this day, though Kareem respects the boxer's right to his own beliefs and opinions, he calls him "Cassius X."

When the 1971–1972 NBA season opened, all eyes were on the Milwaukee Bucks and Kareem Abdul-Jabbar. As defending champions and reigning MVP, they were expected to continue as the powerhouses of the Western Division. But changes had taken place over the summer elsewhere in that division, notably in Los Angeles where the Lakers, with one of the oldest starting five in pro basketball would, under their new coach Bill Sharman, start to run and develop one of the most devastating fast breaks in the league. The Lakers finished the regular season with a 69–13 won-lost record, the best in NBA history, and placed first in the league's Western Division. Milwaukee finished in second place.

Still, it had been another excellent year for Kareem. In regular season play he had led the league with a scoring average of 34.8 points per game and finished third in rebounding with a 16.6 average. For the second year in a row, he was named the league's Most Valuable Player. But individual achievement is not paramount in a team sport, and no matter what laurels Abdul-Jabbar won, they could not make up, even in his own mind, for the failure of his team to hold onto the NBA championship. The Bucks lost to the Lakers in the semi-finals, four games to two, and retired their basketballs considerably earlier that spring than they had planned. The Lakers went on to beat the New York Knicks in the championship series.

That spring Kareem and Habiba became the parents of a daughter whom they also named Habiba. Pride in his new daughter helped to take the edge off his team's loss in the semi-finals, and indeed Kareem did not fret long about losing the championship. Basketball was only one part of his life. An equally important part was his faith. He practiced it every day, facing Mecca and saying his prayers the requisite five times, but when he was not involved in the grueling schedule of the Bucks' season, he had more time to devote to advancing the cause of Islam. He felt it was his duty to do so both by proselytizing and by sharing some of his worldly success.

Fall seemed to arrive very quickly, and with it the requisite Bucks' practice sessions to get summer-sluggish players back into shape for the pre-season exhibition games and then the regular season. It would be the first pre-season experience with the Bucks for new general manager Wayne Embry. Signed by the Milwaukee management the previous spring, Embry, a former pro basketball star himself, was the first black to be signed to a managerial position on an NBA team. As such, he would be watched closely by both supporters and detractors, a fact he acknowledged with equanimity. He would do the best he could with what he had. Kareem Abdul-Jabbar was one supporter who asked no more of his team's GM than that. But what

Embry had to work with turned out to be considerably less than what he, or anyone else for that matter, expected. The natural expectation was that he would have a full roster of players, but for one reason or another that did not prove to be the case. A combination of factors depleted both the physical strength and the psychological well-being of many Bucks players that 1972–1973 season.

It all started during the pre-season exhibition period. Following a game in Denver with the ABA Denver Nuggets, Lucius Allen was arrested on suspicion of marijuana possession. Authorities claimed traces of the drug had been found in a bag Allen was carrying. Allen had been convicted of marijuana possession at U.C.L.A. back in 1968, and the prospect of a second conviction and a possible jail sentence weighed heavily on his mind. Though his on-court performance did not appear to suffer, the psychological burden was difficult to carry. And as the case was continued again and again in the courts, Lucius's problems must have been of concern to his teammates as well, if only because they could result in the loss to the team of an important man.

The Bucks also had numerous medical problems. Oscar Robertson started the season with an aching toe and then developed a deep muscle pull in his shoulder. Favoring the aching parts of his body, he did not render his traditionally fine performance, and around the basketball world the whispers began that perhaps the thirty-four-year-old star was washed up.

Two months into the 1972–1973 season, guard Wali Jones was placed on indefinite medical suspension. The officially announced reason was that he had lost weight and stamina, but at the same time it was announced that Jones had been placed on a thirty-day suspension for violation of curfew and other misconduct. Whatever the published statements, clearly neither the Bucks management nor Jones was content with their relationship. Later Jones was put on waivers, meaning that the Bucks no longer wanted him and any team that wanted him could have him.

There were other injuries, and other evidences of dissension on the team. By the middle of February, team injuries had been so rampant that coach Larry Costello was lamenting that he had enjoyed a full roster for only one game the entire season. Fortunately, the Bucks could be certain of having Lucius Allen around. Early in February the charges of possession of marijuana were dropped because of insufficient evidence. Relieved of worry over the case, Lucius would go on to play some of his finest pro games.

Despite their injuries and assorted other problems, the Milwaukee Bucks were holding their own in the NBA with a 41–18 won-lost record, and Kareem was close to the top among league-leading scorers even though he was not playing with a full Bucks starting team most of the time. But although Kareem averaged 30.2 points per game during the regular season, Nate Archibald, guard for the Kansas City-Omaha Kings, finished the 1972–1973 season with a 34-point average. Kareem's individual averages aside, the important thing was that his team, despite their problems, managed to finish the season with a 60–22 record. This was exactly the same record as that of the defending NBA champions, the Los Angeles Lakers.

Usually a team's won-lost record determines which team it will play in the conference playoffs. In the case of the Bucks and the Lakers, a coin toss was decisive. Los Angeles lost the toss and thus had to play the Chicago Bulls, who had the next best record in the NBA Western Division. The Bucks would face the fourth-place team, the Golden State Warriors. The Warriors had won only forty-seven games during regular season play, and it appeared that the Bucks had drawn the easier series.

Not so. The Warriors eliminated the Bucks from further playoff contention, beating them in the series four games to two. A lot of factors contributed to this result, but one stood out above the others. The Warriors' Nate Thurmond was assigned to guard Kareem Abdul-Jabbar, and throughout the series he held Kareem to a point total well below his season average. Kareem was unhappily reminded of the first time, as a rookie, he had played against Thurmond —the more experienced player had embarrassed him thoroughly. The match-up was nowhere near as uneven this time, and Kareem's scores—22 points, 19 points, 25 points—were point totals of which most pro basketball players would have been proud. But for Kareem Abdul-Jabbar they were not satisfactory. Indeed, toward the end of the series with the Warriors the word "lackadaisical" began to be heard from his coaches, some of his fellow players, and some sportswriters.

The Warriors had beaten the Bucks! It was an upset of almost historic proportions. Coach Larry Costello muttered that his team had at times numbered not five men, but four, and insiders knew that he was implying a lack of effort on the part of his center. The term used in basketball circles to describe a conscious lack of effort is "dogging it." It is not likely that Kareem, the professional player who has been among the most open in describing pro basketball as a job and describing himself as a man who is paid highly to do his job, was actually "dogging it" during that series. The problem, if it can be identified at all and if it was not simply a matter of a superior defensive effort on the part of Nate Thurmond, was probably a lack of concentration. Even one who has consciously tried to discipline his mind in the way Kareem has cannot completely control his ability to concentrate. Had Kareem announced that he wanted to be traded to another team at the end of the season, the charge that he was dogging it might have been appropriate, but he had not made such an announcement. It might have been appropriate, too, if he had publicly expressed dissatisfaction with his Milwaukee contract, but he had not. If Kareem was not playing his best during the playoffs with the Warriors, it is unlikely that this was deliberate. And when the Bucks' disappointment over losing the series abated, there was no more talk implying that Kareem had not done the best he could.

Happily, Wayne Embry's job was not jeopardized by the poor team showing in the playoffs either, nor was that of any of the other people in coaching or managerial positions with the franchise. The Milwaukee Bucks organization sighed and figured things had to be better next season.

When the 1973–1974 pre-season practices began, Kareem returned to his team prepared to contribute both physically and mentally. Since the rest of the Bucks were healthy, they were looking forward to a fine season and were determined to go all the way to the championship.

Kareem played superbly that season. He and Lucius Allen meshed perfectly once more. Other Bucks set up plays for him, feeding their center the ball, and he took advantage of them all. By the end of the regular season, Milwaukee had captured another division title and Kareem Abdul-Jabbar would be voted the NBA's most valuable player once again. He was almost universally acknowledged as the finest center in the game.

The Bucks knew only too well that winning their division was a far cry from winning the league title, and when Lucius Allen got hurt and was unable to play, the road to the championship suddenly loomed long and full of pitfalls. But the rest of the Bucks stepped in and in the next few weeks the Milwaukee team looked so strong in the playoffs that most observers believed they would be hard for any team to stop from going all the way. Despite the absence of Allen, the Bucks rolled over both Los Angeles and Chicago, winning eight of the nine games they played in the two series. But the finals would not be so easy. The Bucks faced the mighty Boston Celtics. The Boston team had not been in the finals since 1969, and nothing was going to stop them from regaining the crown they had held so long during their golden era.

It promised to be an exciting series. The acknowledged two top clubs in the league could not have had less similar styles. Milwaukee relied on its big men and on patience, and carefully worked out plays to get the ball to them. Boston was a smaller team; its game was faster, depending on a pressure defense and the fast break on offense. The league's best center, Kareem Abdul-Jabbar, would be matched up against the NBA's second-best, Dave Cowens. Back in Cowens' rookie year, Kareem had scored 53 points against him in a single game. Cowens had felt foolish,

In the 1974 NBA playoff finals between the Milwaukee Bucks and the Boston Celtics, Kareem, the league's best center, was matched against Dave Cowens, second-best center in the NBA. Despite a fine individual series for Kareem, Boston won the league championship four games to three.

United Press International Photo

and he was determined to outplay the Bucks' big center in this series.

The 1974 finals began in early May, in Boston. In the absence of Allen, other Bucks were assigned the task of feeding the ball to Kareem. They managed to do so, but the Boston pressure was effective nevertheless. Abdul-Jabbar would get the ball just in time for a quick shot, but not in time for his teammates to get in for the rebound and shots of their own if he missed. Kareem still scored 35 points, but the next highest Milwaukee player point total was 12. Boston won the game, 98–83.

In the second game, at Milwaukee, Coach Costello decided to assign Oscar Robertson the sole responsibility for getting the ball upcourt, thereby allowing other Bucks more time to get into position near the basket. But the Boston pressure forced Milwaukee into making twenty-two costly turnovers. Fortunately, Kareem made up for them. In addition to scoring 36 points, he set most of the picks and threw most of the passes. And he made a play that probably was the key to the entire game. With seconds to go and the score tied, Dave Cowens got the ball and drove to the basket with a running hook that certainly would have gone in, had not Abdul-Jabbar leaped out of nowhere to make one of the cleanest and most decisive blocks anyone has ever seen. Milwaukee went on to win the game in overtime, 105–96.

Milwaukee continued to be plagued by costly turnovers, and with its game so dependent on one man,

Abdul-Jabbar, the team was in trouble when the Celtics found a combination that would slow down the Bucks' key player. Despite the pressure, Kareem turned in some memorable performances, but Boston had such depth, so much help for its big man, Cowens, that they outlasted the Milwaukee team. The series was close, and many basketball buffs called it the finest they had seen in ten years. Teams roared back from huge deficits, favorites lost, the home court advantage did not seem to make a difference, but in the end the Celtics won the series four games to three and once again Kareem Abdul-Jabbar found himself a champion on a non-championship team. Some reporters pointed out that the same problem had plagued Wilt Chamberlain, who would defend himself by saying he was not getting enough help from his teammates. "Do you sometimes feel the same way?" they asked Kareem, but he would not be baited. "You're trying to get me to say that my teammates aren't any good," he would say. "I have no comment on that."

Oscar Robertson retired at the end of that season. He was thirty-five years old. Though he had slowed down, he still had some good playing years ahead of him, but the Bucks' management wanted to take the no-cut clause out of his contract and he was afraid he would indeed be cut eventually if he agreed to the change. One thing he did not want to do was to be told when to leave basketball. So, he quit. Several other members of the Bucks were traded. By the time pre-season exhibition games began in the fall of 1974, only Kareem, Bobby Dandridge, and Lucius Allen remained as starters who were familiar with and practiced in the Bucks' intricate offense.

As a rule, pre-season games do not inspire great excitement. Real basketball buffs follow them closely, looking for harbingers of the season to come, but most sports fans are still going to football games and following the World Series in baseball. The Bucks played one exhibition game, however, that engendered real excitement, for it was the first match-up between two former U.C.L.A. star centers, Kareem Abdul-Jabbar and Bill Walton.

Abdul-Jabbar was four years older than Walton, so the two had never played together at U.C.L.A. But in his sophomore year Walton had begun to exhibit the kind of skill as a center that U.C.L.A. had not seen since the Alcindor days, and naturally comparisons between the two began to be made and continued throughout Walton's college days. Kareem declined to comment on Walton's basketball prowess, but in unguarded moments he was heard to remark about Walton's relationship with John Wooden. During his school career, Kareem had always had intense relationships with his coaches, and he still recalled with a trace of bitterness the seemingly impenetrable barrier that had existed between him and Wooden, the barrier of race. He had read about Bill Walton's somewhat nonconformist ways—his left-wing politics, his liking for marijuana—and could not help resenting that although he had not indulged such habits, he had never enjoyed with Wooden the close relationship Walton and the coach seemed to share. "There was warm, mutual respect between Wooden and me," Kareem once said. "But because I was black there was never the father-son thing he had going with Bill Walton. He couldn't put his arm around my waist and introduce me as his boy—we didn't look very much alike. He could do it with Walton. Now I think that John regrets it. Walton has turned out to be such a crybaby because he got away with murder then. It was so bad that Walton once said he wouldn't show up for practice unless he was allowed to smoke grass in the locker room—that's where Wooden drew the line."

In other words, when Kareem Abdul-Jabbar, veteran of the Milwaukee Bucks, and Bill Walton, rookie on the Portland Trail Blazers, met on court for the first time in October 1974, their rivalry was more than purely professional. Walton did not talk much, but no doubt it was in his mind that he had always been in the shadow of the man who had been called Lew Alcindor. He had finished second-highest scorer in U.C.L.A. history, behind Alcindor.

Game time arrived. The 6'11" Walton loped onto the floor not exactly looking like a charter member of the NBA, his long red hair held in place by a sweatband, his beard an equally flaming color.

Kareem played him cautiously at first, trying to feel out the younger man. A full two minutes went by before he made his first shot, a short jumper. It went in. Then he went to work. In seemingly rapid succession he made a stuff, another jumper, a lay-up and a hook, and with one second left in the first quarter he grabbed a loose ball about 15 feet away from the basket and casually hit with his famous sky hook. The buzzer sounded, but Bill Walton remained on the floor, staring at the basket, then at the spot from which Kareem had shot, then back at the basket, shaking his head. Three quarters later, the Bucks had won, 103–96, and their center had far outscored their opponents' man. Abdul-Jabbar had racked up 34 points, Walton 15. During the twenty-seven minutes they were on the floor together, Kareem had outscored his younger opponent 28–8.

But Abdul-Jabbar was not underestimating Walton. He had taken note of the rebound statistics, Walton's 16 to his 11. He had seen Walton slapping those offensive rebounds away to keep the ball in play for his team, looking to set up a teammate with a good pass instead of going to the basket himself. He remembered his own first match-up as a rookie against Nate Thurmond and how badly he'd been beaten. He thought Walton had done okay, and he had a new respect for the younger man. In his hotel room after the game, Kareem lay on his bed and watched television with some friends. When the wrap-up of the game came on, the sportscaster started talking about how Abdul-Jabbar had outplayed Walton. Kareem looked up at the ceiling and sighed, "Big deal."

The next night Kareem Abdul-Jabbar lost his cool. In another exhibition game he went up for a ball, crashed into his opponent, and came down with a scratched left eye. He was outraged. He had suffered several eye injuries before, and nothing scared him more than the prospect of permanent damage. Why did this have to happen? He wanted to hit the man who had injured him. Instead, he hit the backboard post—and broke his hand.

Now he was furious at himself. "How could I have done anything so stupid?" he asked the team's trainer Bill Bates. "Why do ten million people kick wastebaskets?" Bates replied. But that did not console Kareem. Ten million people had not studied prayer and meditation as long as he had. He fingered the Islamic star and crescent that he wore around his neck and wondered what had happened, that moment out there on the court, to the inner peace he had striven so hard to attain. He had forgotten that basketball was just a job. Now he would not be able to play for several weeks, and his major injury was self-inflicted.

The hand healed. So did the eye. But Kareem was taking no more chances. His eyes were just in the range of his opponents' fingernails, and they were bound to be injured again unless he took steps to protect them. Already there was some scarring in the whites of the eyes because of repeated injuries; they could not take further injury. Early in December, basketball fans were astonished to see trotting out onto the court what looked like a 7'2" space man in shorts. Kareem Abdul-Jabbar had become the first and only professional basketball player to wear wrap-around goggles of the sort that the Wright brothers wore at Kitty Hawk. Made of bright yellow Plexiglas, they quickly earned him the nickname "Old Google Eyes." He had expected some ribbing and was prepared for it, and he preferred a few jokes to another injury. After a while, people got used to his appearance, and Kareem's space goggles gradually became as non-noteworthy as his new name.

At first, however, they were hard to get used to for everyone concerned, including Kareem. In fact, he was supposed to have returned to the Bucks' lineup one game earlier than he actually did. The team was on a road trip and Kareem was to join them in a game against Kansas City. He arrived in time for the game, only to discover that he had forgotten to pack his goggles. A hasty call was made to the Bucks' public relations director back in Milwaukee, and he went over to Kareem's apartment to get the glasses. He couldn't find them. He called the press table at the Kansas City arena and Kareem got on the telephone and suggested various places to look. At last he remembered that he'd left them in his black Mercedes. "It was unreal," recalled trainer Bill Bates. "Here a game is going on and we're yelling back and forth for a full quarter trying to find the goggles." By then, of course, it was too late to get the glasses all the way to Kansas City, so Kareem sat on the bench that night.

His return to the court took place in New York in a game against the Knicks. Cornell Warner started in the center position, but after Knicks center John Gianelli scored five quick points against Warner, Coach Costello sent Kareem in. After that, Gianelli scored just four more points. Kareem scored seventeen, grabbed ten rebounds, and blocked four shots. The Bucks won, 90–72.

Kareem was still out of shape. He was finding it hard to get used to playing with the goggles on and was not particularly happy with their design because they blocked his peripheral vision. But he had no second thoughts about continuing to wear goggles. As he put it, "I'm down to my last pair of eyeballs." New goggles, three inches wider and with harder-coated lenses, would prove much more satisfactory.

The Bucks had compiled a dismal record during Kareem's absence. After he had been injured, the team had found itself not just lacking its star center but without any center at all. Dick Cunningham, who was supposed to function as Kareem's alternate, was injured himself. They moved forward Cornell Warner into the center position and brought in Walt Wesley, whom the Philadelphia 76ers had put on waivers, as his back-up. But the Bucks were still losing. None of their guards could bring the ball upcourt the way Oscar Robertson had. Lucius Allen had been expected to take over Robertson's old job, but he did not seem able to do it, and in November the Bucks shocked a lot of people by trading Allen to the Los Angeles Lakers in exchange for Jim Price. Allen was shocked; he had expected to stay with the Bucks for a while. The fans were shocked—Allen and Abdul-Jabbar played so well together. Kareem was shocked—he'd played with Allen since college; the two were good friends and fine teammates. He did not like the idea of having to get used to yet more new Bucks players when he returned.

The Bucks lost their next game, against Los Angeles, but won the following two, against Kansas City-Omaha and Chicago. Their season record was now 6–14. Half of their wins had come since the return of Abdul-Jabbar, which indicates how sorely he was missed. On the other hand, his teammates had enjoyed getting the chance to take more shots. With Kareem back, they would return to the old pattern of feeding the ball to their star center. As forward Bobby Dandridge explained, "The problem when Kareem plays is that seventy-five percent of our offense goes to him. You know that when the ball goes in the middle he's going to hook or take some kind of shot. Then everybody isn't totally involved on offense. It tends to make guys not enthusiastic."

The new men, like George Thompson who had come over from the ABA, were used to taking more shots. They found it hard to alter their playing styles seventeen games into the season. There were so many new players for Kareem to get used to and who, in turn, had to adjust to him. Had the season just begun, they might have been able to find the right blend and Kareem would have gotten back into top shape in time to lead his team to a playoff position. But the season was well along. Kareem got back into shape and finished the season with a 29.9 points per game average. Though it brought his career average down to 30.4, it was still the highest of any player career average in NBA history. And his field goal average of 55 percent was still the best in the history of the league. But the Bucks never got together as a team well enough to make the playoffs, and for the first time since Kareem had joined the Milwaukee team, basketball for the Bucks players was over at the end of the regular season.

That was not all that was over for Kareem. His marriage had soured. The pressures of being the wife of a professional athlete had been too much for Habiba, and other pressures had taken their toll as well. Habiba went back to Washington, D.C., taking their three-year-old daughter with her.

Kareem decided it was time to leave Milwaukee. He had never liked the city anyway—the weather was lousy. He was unhappy with the team, with carrying the entire franchise on his back. He was tired of the other players' thinly disguised resentment. He missed his old teammates—Oscar Robertson and especially Lucius. He wanted to go to a new city and a new team but not just anywhere. He had always wanted to play for the New York Knicks and live in Manhattan where he had grown up. Through his agent he let it be known to the Milwaukee management that he wanted to be traded, and to the Knicks management that he was open to offers.

The Knicks made an offer, but it was not what Kareem considered "responsible." He was the best center in basketball, and he was not about to sell himself cheap no matter how much he wanted to play for New York. But no further offers were forthcoming from the Knicks, so Kareem turned his attention to the bids from other teams. The Bucks management, meanwhile, was doing its own negotiating. They certainly did not want an unhappy player, so they were willing to trade Abdul-Jabbar, even though he was the key to the franchise. But they wanted appropriate compensation—players and money in exchange for their star. The best offer came from the Los Angeles Lakers, and the Bucks decided to take it. For his part, Kareem decided Los Angeles was probably his second choice. Everyone being relatively satisfied, the deal was made, and Kareem, for whom Lakers owner Jack Kent had, as one sportswriter put it, "traded his estate plus the better part of downtown Inglewood," was playing for a Los Angeles team again after a six-year absence.

For Kareem and Lucius Allen, it was just like old times. They had to laugh. No matter what happend, they always seemed to wind up playing on the same team. They visited some of their old college haunts together, and Lucius helped Kareem get settled and find a place to live. Kareem moved into a ranch house in Stone Canyon above the U.C.L.A. campus. He chose it partly because of its cathedral ceilings, which gave him a feeling of space he rarely enjoyed. Though it already had a pool and a paddle-tennis court, he planned to add a tennis practice area, among other things. He did not intend to move again soon.

5
A Laker for Life

THE TEAM WITH WHICH KAREEM HAD SIGNED A FIVE-year contract was in a period of decline. They had at least made their division playoffs for the preceding three years. Indeed, they had won the NBA championship in 1972. But their starting lineup was composed of older players, and as they retired the Lakers had to replace them with less experienced or less skilled men. Going into the 1975–1976 season, the team's roster looked like a "Who's Nobody" list, except for Kareem and a few others. Their guards, Lucius Allen and Gail Goodrich, were too small to go up against the big guards of other teams. Their forwards had little offensive power. To make matters worse, the coaching staff was not united. Head coach Bill Sharman was not tough enough either to take a player out when he was not producing or to keep his assistant coaches in line. It all portended a disastrous season, and that is exactly the type of season through which the Lakers suffered. There were no fewer than seventeen starting lineup changes. The coaching was equally confused; there were times when the players found themselves under conflicting orders from several assistant coaches. The Lakers did not even make the playoffs. They finished in fourth place in their division with a 40–42 record.

But the team's troubles were no reflection on Kareem. Individually, he had enjoyed a fine season. He had finished first in the league in rebounding with 1,383, an average of 16.9 per game, and second to Buffalo's Bob McAdoo in individual scoring with 2,275 points, or 27.7 per game. He was voted the league's most valuable player for the fourth time in his six-year professional career. He would have preferred being on a winning team. But there was always next season, and Kareem had other things to think about. After completing business at home, he took off for Pakistan to conduct a basketball clinic and polish up the journalism skills he had learned in college. After all, he could not play basketball forever. He thought he just might go into writing as a second career.

While Kareem was away, a lot of changes were made, not just in the Lakers organization but in the structure of professional basketball as well. The struggling ABA had folded. The newer league had started the 1975–1976 season with nine teams, but by the end of the season only four were financially sound. Four teams were not enough for a viable league. The ABA and the NBA had been talking merger for a couple of years, and now merger was the only way to keep the remaining ABA teams in business. So, in the fall of 1976 four new teams would be on the NBA's schedule: the New York Nets, the San Antonio Spurs, the Denver Nuggets, and the Indiana Pacers. Many of the players from now-defunct former ABA teams were available to NBA teams and were signed on by, among other teams, the Los Angeles Lakers. All this new talent meant that some not-so-skilled NBA players would lose their jobs, and that nearly every NBA player would have to work harder to keep his job.

The NBA–ABA merger had another ramification. A new scheduling system was established. There were twenty-two teams and under the new schedule each team would play each of the other teams four times, two games at home and two games on their opponents' court. It all seemed very fair, and on paper it somehow worked out, but basketball players are more than symbols on a sheet of paper. The new schedule required long road trips, sometimes as long as eighteen days, and even short trips are not easy on a team. Planes are late, taxis are scarce, baggage gets lost or misdirected, hotel rooms are barren, and beds are usually too short. Jet lag riles the stomach, and road trip food is miserable anyway. Not a few observers were predicting that the NBA championship would be decided in large measure not on the basis of skill but on that of road trip endurance, and no team was expected to win more than a fraction of its road trip games.

As for the changes in the Lakers organization, they were many and comprehensive. Six players were cut or traded. Gail Goodrich was replaced by former

ABA defensive specialist Don Chaney. Cornell Warner, Stu Lantz, Cliff Meely, Don Freeman and Jim McDaniels were all cut, replaced by two rookies, Tom Abernathy and Earl Tatum, and three other former ABA players, Bo Lamar, Johnny Neumann and Marv Roberts. The coaching staff had been re-vamped as well. Bill Sharman was now General Manager. In his place, the Lakers organization hired former NBA all-pro star Jerry West to his first coaching job. "When he got the job," Kareem recalls, "he called me up and told me he thought we could win, that we could have fun."

Jerry West believed in real team play, in cooperation and helping. He gave his coaching staff a share of the coaching responsibilities, but each assistant had specific duties that did not conflict with the others'. He used the same philosophy in choosing his starting lineup. Unlike Milwaukee's Coach Costello, he did not want Abdul-Jabbar to play as if he were the only offensive man on the court. Much of the offense would be patterned around him, but not to the exclusion of the rest of the good shooters, particularly the outside shooters. Lucius Allen had an excellent outside shot, as did veteran Cazzie Russell and rookie Earl Tatum. West established a structured defense, what he called a "helping defense," in which the Lakers spread out on the court to give their three outside shooters picks and screens in the spots from which they liked to shoot. He also gave 6'8" Kermit Washington the responsibility of relieving Abdul-

Jabbar of some of the defensive pressure he always got.

In theory, it sounded great; in pre-season practice, it worked well. But West was expecting no miracles. Neither were most basketball observers. Just because West had been a superb player did not mean he would be a good coach. Just because the Lakers were largely a brand new team did not mean they could blend their skills and create a new image. As a matter of fact, despite the presence of Abdul-Jabbar, they were expected to finish the season in at least the bottom half of the league. Opponents' scouts reported back, "There isn't much talent there. It's just Abdul-Jabbar and a bunch of guys."

The quality Jerry West stressed most was intelligence. He expected his players to work hard, even to overexert themselves when the situation called for it, but never to get so excited that they made foolish mistakes. That was the kind of play that suited Abdul-Jabbar. He also appreciated West's efforts at achieving more balance on the team. The presence of Kermit Washington relieved him of some of the pressure defense that he used to describe as "the

Kareem scrambles after the ball while being double-teamed by the Denver Nuggets in a November 1976 game. The early part of the 1976–77 season was a time of rebuilding for the Lakers with new coach Jerry West and a largely brand new team. By mid-November the Lakers had become a working unit and a strong contender in the NBA's Pacific Division.

United Press International Photo

101st Airborne on my back." With other players encouraged to shoot, he could use his pivotal position to make key passes when he did not have a good shot himself. He even got a chance to develop further his already awesome shooting. He added to his list of shots a turnaround jumper that came to be called the "moonball." It took a while for the players to mesh, but by mid-November of 1976 the Lakers had themselves a real team, and from then on they became powerful contenders in the toughest division in the NBA, the Pacific. By mid-February, fifty games into the season, they were enjoying a 33–17 record, and had won 20 in a row on their home court and an unbelievable 9 games on the road.

"I'm happy again," Kareem told reporters. "Winning makes me happy. It's what made Milwaukee tolerable. Last year we never got anything done. I was not optimistic in the pre-season. But Jerry came in and organized, which I could not anticipate. Without arrogance, he was frank in what he wanted to do."

Winning was not the only source of Kareem's happiness. He really liked being in California. The weather was great, he enjoyed his new home, and he had matured to the point of being able to relax and enjoy

Sporting the protective goggles he has worn in every game since his eye injury in a pre-season exhibition game in the fall of 1975, Kareem lets fly one of his newer shots against the Boston Celtics in November 1976. Sportswriters call the turnaround jump shot a "moonball" in an obvious reference to Kareem's spaceman-like headgear.

United Press International Photo

the casual lifestyle. He was more willing to talk to reporters, to sign autographs. In response, sportswriters were more generous in their assessment of his personality, and advertising concerns dared to approach him to seek his endorsement of commercial products. He appeared on TV advertisements for talcum powder and orange juice, and did guest spots on such shows as *Mannix* and *Emergency!* Such activities earned him considerable sums of money, and he had never made any secret of the fact that a major reason for his being in professional basketball was the money. Still, he loved the game, and the good feeling he had about his team and his new manager made him love it even more. That season, he sometimes got that old exhilarating feeling that he had felt as a youngster—the kind of feeling that caused him to do joyful things like slapping palms with Jerry West or throwing a basketball rafterward after a close victory. His statistics so far that season were cause for joy as well. He led the NBA in shooting percentage and was second in scoring, rebounding, and blocked shots.

Some observers believed the presence of Bill Walton might have contributed to Kareem's superb playing. Games between the Los Angeles Lakers and the Portland Trail Blazers had become *the* games for West Coast fans to see, and the match-up between the two big, powerful centers a classic one, reminiscent of that between Wilt Chamberlain and Bill Russell. Walton had matured considerably as a player since the last season, and although Abdul-Jabbar still outplayed him he could no longer do so easily. A real competitor thrives on real competition, and Kareem was at his best when playing against Walton.

By midseason, the two teams had met three times and the Lakers had won all three contests by 3, 4, and 5 points. Walton had missed one game because of an inflamed Achilles tendon, but the other two games had been among the most exciting of the NBA season. Abdul-Jabbar had piled up 67 points and 30 rebounds against Walton's 54 points and 47 rebounds. Their competition was one of the most balanced between two players in the history of the NBA, and as the season came to a close it became clear that the rivalry would continue into the post-season. The two top teams in the NBA Pacific Division would oppose each other in a best 4 out of 7 playoff series. The coming competition was the talk of the league. Walton and Abdul-Jabbar were not among the talkers, however. "I'm excited," was about all Walton would say. "It's a challenge," said Kareem.

Odds makers favored Portland. Although Los Angeles had a better season record (their 53 wins, 29 losses was the best record in the league), they had less depth than the Blazers. Jerry West had tried to come up with a more balanced team, but Abdul-Jabbar still bore the overwhelming offensive responsibility, not to mention a sizable share of the defense. Then, too, the Lakers had two key men on the injury list. The powerful Kermit Washington, who was so

important in taking the defensive pressure off Kareem, was out for all post-season play, and Lucius Allen had a dislocated toe. He was the most unlucky man— one injury or another always seemed to keep him out of the important games. He did not even suit up for the first game. By contrast, the Blazers were all healthy, and though Bill Walton was without doubt their key man, all season he had received far more help from his teammates than had Abdul-Jabbar.

Because the Lakers had the better regular season record, the first two games were played at the Forum in Los Angeles. The two teams met for the opener one evening in early May. The Lakers got off to a bad start. Blazers worked a pressing defense on Abdul-Jabbar and allowed him only two points the entire first quarter. Other Lakers did not step in to take up the slack. By the end of the first half Portland was ahead 61–43, and the Lakers never did catch up. Though Kareem scored 30 points, the Lakers lost 121–109 on their home court, something they were not in the habit of doing.

Los Angeles lost the second game at the Forum as well. This time Kareem worked even harder and scored 40 points as well as pulling down 17 rebounds,

Kareem roars to the basket through a crowd of New York Knicks in a game in Los Angeles January 21, 1977. Happy about his team's fourteen-game winning streak, Kareem was also personally content for the first time in some years. He was also enjoying the best relationship he had ever had with sportswriters. *United Press International Photo* but Walton forced him into a bad shot for the game-tying basket and Portland won the game 99–97. By this time, many fans were wondering how the Lakers had managed to win so many games during the regular season.

Of course they were playing without Lucius Allen and Kermit Washington, but their healthy players were not producing either. Cazzie Russell was shooting a dismal 39 percent. Earl Tatum had scored 32 points in the first game but did little thereafter. Even the Lakers' defense seemed helpless against the Blazers' fast break. More and more pressure was put on Abdul-Jabbar. Jerry West didn't like it, but he knew he did not have the depth Blazer coach Jack Ramsay enjoyed. "Excluding the big guys, would you want our eleven [players] or their eleven?" he snapped at a sportswriter who was trying to get him to say something controversial. "I have to feel sorry for Kareem. It's a terrible burden we put on him." Kareem said simply, "I like the way the Blazers play. They should be national champs."

The third game, played in Portland, looked like

The Lakers had finished the regular season with a better won-lost record than had the Trail Blazers. As the playoff semifinals began, however, two key Los Angeles players were sidelined with injuries. Kareem was under great pressure to carry his team's effort, despite frequent triple-teaming by Maurice Lucas, Bill Walton, and Lionel Hollins.

United Press International Photo

the comeback chance for the Lakers. Lucius Allen returned, and although he was still unable to run well, his presence seemed to spark his teammates. With 9:10 left to play, the Lakers led 81–77. Abdul-Jabbar had been all over the court, shooting, passing, defending. Walton had scored only 8 points. Then, suddenly, Walton erupted. Playing as if Abdul-Jabbar were not even on the court, he made seven baskets in the next five minutes, stuffing, hooking, banking, tipping. Portland took the lead, 93–84, and by the end of the game the Blazers had won their third straight, 102–97.

To say the least, the statistics were against the Lakers. It would be almost impossible for the team to come from an 0–3 deficit to win the playoff series. But Kareem Abdul-Jabbar was one Laker who was willing to give his all to the effort. The fourth game was marked by very aggressive action under the boards, but late in the third quarter Kareem committed his fourth and fifth fouls and was forced to go to the bench. At the time, the Lakers were ahead by three points. When he returned, the Blazers were out in front by six.

This was it, thought Kareem. They were minutes away from losing the playoff series in four straight games—or from keeping their hopes alive by winning at least one game. He turned into a whirlwind defensive player, batting away every inside shot the Blazers took. On the other end of the court, he made or set up shots that brought the Lakers to within two points.

But Portland made two more points on an outside shot. The buzzer sounded. The score was 105–101. It was all over for the Lakers.

After the three earlier games, Walton and Abdul-Jabbar had sought each other out and clasped hands, congratulating each other on a good game played. Not this night. Kareem rushed from the floor as the Trail Blazers' fans spilled out of the stands to celebrate the victory of their team. Blazer Maurice Lucas took a moment to watch the receding figure. "Jabbar would never give up," he remarked. "He's the most respected player in the league because he never bows his head. Such great inner strength! You may beat his team but you never beat him."

The series statistics bore out Lucas's statement. Kareem Abdul-Jabbar had played a tremendous series: 121 points in 61 percent shooting, 64 rebounds, and 15 blocked shots. He had outdone every one of Walton's comparative statistics—77 points, 50 percent shooting, 59 rebounds, and 9 blocked shots. But Walton had not been forced to play as if he were alone on the court; there were many times when Kareem had. Too often during the season the Laker game had been a one-on-five situation, Kareem against the opposing team. It may have worked then; it did not work in consecutive games against a well-balanced team with Bill Walton as its center.

Walton and the Portland Trail Blazers went on to beat the Philadelphia 76ers to win the NBA championship. Abdul-Jabbar hung up his basketball sneakers for yet another season, but it had been a season of which he could be proud. He had led the league in field goal percentage (.579), was third in scoring (26.2 points per game), second in rebounding (13.3), and second in blocked shots (3.18), and when his fellow professionals sat down to vote for the man whom they considered the best in the league, it was Kareem Abdul-Jabbar they thought of. By a vote of 159 to 29, the players of the National Basketball Association selected him as the league's most valuable player for the second year in a row and for the fifth time in his career. Only one other man, Bill Russell of the Boston Celtics, had been selected to receive the award five times, and Abdul-Jabbar still had several seasons left to play.

He was thirty years old, which is getting on in the pounding, driving, up-and-down-the-court-racing game of basketball. But he was also an experienced, mature player. "I have more understanding of the game," he says. "The little things you have to do well. When to switch, when not to. When to help out, when not to. When to pass, when to hold the ball." He was, in the opinion of the experts, playing better than ever, and he heartily agreed with this assessment.

Kareem dunks against Portland. Individually, he played a brilliant series, but he got too little help from his teammates against the aggressive, running game of the Trail Blazers. Portland won the series 4–0.

United Press International Photo

That spring and summer, changes on the team indicated that in the next season, Abdul-Jabbar might not have to carry the franchise himself. The series with Portland had clearly shown the Lakers' need for more rebounding and greater speed, and coach West had made some key trades and deals with individual players to meet those needs. New Lakers included Jamaal Wilkes, formerly of the Golden State Warriors, Ernie DiGregorio of the Buffalo Braves and Lou Hudson of the Atlanta Hawks, as well as two promising rookies chosen in the college draft. The result was a Laker team with so much depth that three starters from the previous season would probably not start in the fall of 1977. One other starter would not even be with the team. Lucius Allen had been traded once again, this time to the Kansas City-Omaha Kings. Since college, he had played on two teams and now would play on a third. Since college, he and Abdul-Jabbar had always seemed to wind up on the same team, but the habit would not continue—unless Allen is traded back to the Lakers at some point in the future.

Unexpectedly, Kareem Abdul-Jabbar was absent from the Lakers lineup for most of the games during the fall of 1977. In a game against Milwaukee on October 18, 1977, the physical jockeying for position between Kareem and Milwaukee's rookie center, Kent Benson, got out of hand. Receiving an elbow in his stomach, Kareem lost his temper and punched Benson in the head. Both were forced to leave the game,

Benson with a swollen eye and a slight concussion and Kareem with a broken hand. Ironically, it was the same hand he had broken by hitting the backboard support after his own eye was injured three years before. Ironically, too, the Milwaukee coach who witnessed the Jabbar-Benson scuffle was Don Nelson, the man who had stuck his finger in Kareem's eye in that game three years earlier.

There would be much arguing about who was at fault in the Jabbar-Benson incident. Kareem felt he had been harassed. Benson felt Kareem had misinterpreted his defensive maneuvers. NBA Commissioner Larry O'Brien looked at films of the game, decided Kareem's was a premeditated, blatant act and, believing that the increasing violence in the NBA must be stopped, levied the largest fine ever charged against an NBA player for on-court violence, $5,000. He would probably have suspended Kareem for a period of time as well, but doctors said Kareem's hand would take at least three weeks to heal and the Commissioner decided that was a sufficiently long time for Kareem to be out of action.

During the next nineteen Lakers games, Kareem nursed his hand and thought about his temper. He regretted losing it in the Milwaukee game, and he regretted not being able to play with his team as they lost many more games than they won during his absence. Still, he knew he would be able to help the Lakers in the future, for back in October, not long before the Benson incident, he had taken an impor-

Though his hand had healed, Kareem wore a protective bandage after he returned to the Lakers lineup. The bandage hindered his shooting somewhat, but he could still sink a lay-up against Bill Walton.

tant and somewhat unusual step. He signed a lifetime contract with the Los Angeles Lakers. Of course, the contract's wording referred to his "playing lifetime"; nevertheless, the contract represented a commitment that not many professional basketball players, not even many thirty-year-old ones, are prepared to make.

And what about after his playing lifetime is over? Kareem is not sure yet, and he is in no hurry to make his decision. He has plenty of options. When he was younger, he once said, "I always liked teaching. Maybe I'll teach. Maybe I'll do social work. Whatever I do, I'm pretty sure it will be with black kids. That's not because I'm prejudiced against white kids. But I was a black kid. I know their scene. I know how to talk to them. I *mean* something to them. . . . The black people need brothers who can express themselves freely and do their own thing, pridefully and manfully. The black people need brothers who have made themselves into something that can be admired, something that can be modeled on."

He has proven himself a fine model. It has taken some time, but people have come to accept him as a sensitive, brave man with deeply felt beliefs on which he is willing to act. His decision to boycott the 1968 Olympics is now viewed generally with respect. He is respected as well for his religious beliefs, and happily his father has come to understand that his taking of a Muslim name was a positive step. Mr. Alcindor now calls his son Kareem. "When he did it I didn't react outwardly," Kareem recalls, "but inside I felt that this was a major victory."

The photograph is deceptive. Seattle Supersonics' center Mike Green is not waving good-by to the ball as Kareem goes up to score. But Kareem, voted NBA's MVP five out of his eight pro seasons, remains one of the most commanding presences on the basketball court.

Wide World Photo

He has acted as well on his belief that black athletes ought to try to share their financial good fortune with the black community. He has talked to other black basketball players about setting up some type of collective economic system that would inject money into the ghettos, and although he has not elicited much interest so far he is still hopeful. Julius Erving of the Philadelphia 76ers shares his dream, and Kareem hopes that the two can work together on some project when they have more time to devote to it.

He would also like to help other children of color. Since his conversion to Islam he has become more aware of and interested in Third World peoples, and has conducted basketball clinics in countries like Pakistan and visited various parts of Arabia and western Africa. He has thought of furthering his causes through journalism, in which he majored in college.

Whatever the future brings, Kareem Abdul-Jabbar is confident of his ability to adjust to life off the basketball court. Although he loves basketball and is grateful for the good life the sport has given him, he is aware that most people still tend to think of him as a giant scoring machine and to emphasize his physical talents. He looks forward to showing and making a contribution with his other talents. As he puts it, "I can do something else besides stuff a ball through a hoop. My biggest resource is my mind."

Index

Italics indicate illustration

CURSES, Inc.

CURSES, Inc.

AND OTHER STORIES

Vivian Vande Velde

JANE YOLEN BOOKS

HARCOURT BRACE & COMPANY

San Diego   New York   London

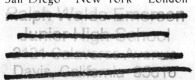

"Past Sunset" copyright © 1996 by Vivian Vande Velde; originally
published in *Bruce Coville's Book of Spine Tinglers* (Scholastic Inc.) edited by
Bruce Coville. "Lost Soul" copyright © 1993 by Vivian Vande Velde;
originally published in *A Wizard's Dozen* (Jane Yolen Books/
Harcourt Brace) edited by Michael Stearns. "Cypress Swamp Granny"
copyright © 1996 by Vivian Vande Velde; originally published in
A Nightmare's Dozen (Jane Yolen Books/Harcourt Brace) edited by
Michael Stearns.

Library of Congress Cataloging-in-Publication Data
Vande Velde, Vivian.
Curses, Inc. and other stories/Vivian Vande Velde.
p.   cm.
"Jane Yolen Books."
Contents: Curses, Inc.—Skin deep—Past sunset—To converse with the
dumb beasts—Boy witch—Lost soul—Remember me—Witch-hunt—
Cypress swamp granny—The witch's son.
ISBN 0-15-201452-7
1. Magic—Juvenile fiction. 2. Children's stories, American. [1. Magic—
Fiction. 2. Short stories.] I. Title.
PZ7.V2773Cu 1997
[Fic]—dc20 96-24856

Text set in Stone Serif
Designed by Judythe Sieck

First edition
A C E F D B

To Karen, in appreciation of all her help and patience.
(Besides, to whom else could I dedicate a collection
of witch stories and be sure she'd
take it the right way?)

CONTENTS

INTRODUCTION:
About That Title...

I'VE ALWAYS HAD A HARD TIME thinking up names for my books.

When I wrote my first novel, *A Hidden Magic,* I found a publishing company that liked the story but not the title. The editor asked for a new one. I sent her a whole list. She didn't like those, either; she asked me to send more. Every time I wrote to her, I sent suggestions. Every time she wrote to me, she asked for more. But in the meanwhile nobody told the illustrator—Trina Schart Hyman—that the book's name was to be changed. She went ahead and did the cover, title and all. Once the editor saw it, she decided the title fit.

The second book I wrote was *Once upon a Test: Three Light Tales of Love.* It was the editor (a different one) who came up with the name.

Third came *A Well-Timed Enchantment,* a title my husband suggested.

I made up the name *User Unfriendly* for my next

book. *I* thought it made sense. My mother—who doesn't use computers, and therefore has no idea just how unfriendly a computer can be—says it's confusing. Perhaps she's right: People are constantly miscalling it *User Friendly*.

When I had no title for book number five, another editor—Jane Yolen—named it *Dragon's Bait* for me.

Companions of the Night was my next book, and I thought the title—my own—was a good one, until somebody pointed out that it sounds as though the story is about a sleazy escort service—which, by the way, it is not.

So I was delighted to have somebody present me with a title for my next book before I even wrote it. I was talking at a school when one of the students suggested I should gather together all the short stories I'd had published in various magazines and publish them in one book. "You could call it," she said, *"A Witch's Stew."*

While I didn't think a collection of old stories would work, I liked the title so much I decided to write some new stories. I took a bunch of familiar fairy tales, turned them upside down, inside out, made the villains be the heroes, the heroes be the villains, created new endings, and sent the collection to Jane Yolen.

Jane said yes to the stories, no to the title. "It doesn't work," she said. "There aren't any witches in this witch's stew."

"But it's more the idea of a *stew*," I explained. "You know: a bunch of things thrown together."

"It doesn't work," she said.

"But did you see how I set up the table of contents like a recipe," I asked, "with the titles of the stories being the ingredients, and instead of saying pages I said tablespoons?"

"Yes," Jane said. "It doesn't work." She suggested *Tales from the Brothers Grimm and the Sisters Weird.*

Even my mother liked Jane's title better than mine.

I sulked. "OK," I told myself. "Jane wants witches; I'll give her witches."

And so I wrote this collection: evil witches, not-so-bad witches, witches from times past, witches on the Internet—a stew of witches.

If you have a good memory, or if you checked back to the cover, you will have noticed that the name of this book is not A Witch's Stew. Jane's work again.

Who knows? Maybe I'll write another book called *A Witch's Stew*, and maybe Jane will accept the book but change the title of that one, too. Maybe we'll keep on doing it. Writers use all kinds of tricks to get or keep themselves writing; maybe writing books not called *A Witch's Stew* will be mine.

CURSES, INC.

BILL ESSLER CAME HOME stamping his feet and slamming doors after Denise Bainbridge humiliated him in front of about half the student population of Thomas Jefferson Junior High.

He had not asked her to go to the eighth-grade graduation dance with him—he knew that for a fact. "Would you *like* to go to the dance with me?"—*that* was what he'd asked back in May when the dance had first been announced. And she'd said, "Yes," and he'd said, "Great," which was close to, but not exactly, the same as saying he actually would take her.

Of course, at the time he, too, had assumed that was what he meant; but since then his mother had said that she and Dad couldn't afford the perfect shirt, pants, and shoes he'd picked out at the mall. And when he pointed out that the family could afford more if Mom would go out and get a job like most of his friends' mothers, she'd gotten all huffy and said he was on his own—not only for the outfit, but for the tickets that she'd originally agreed to pay for, plus the flowers she insisted he needed to buy for Denise.

Bill had the money. Three hundred ninety-five dollars he had—received as Christmas and birthday presents from out-of-town aunts and uncles and saved from working his paper route. With that money he planned to buy the latest computer games to play over the summer. He had no intention of spending a sizable chunk just to take Denise Bainbridge to the eighth-grade dance.

"Would you like to go to the dance with me?" He'd thought about it long and hard and realized it wasn't an invitation but an inquiry into her state of mind. There wasn't a lawyer in the world who could prove that was a binding agreement to take her.

So today he had tried to break it off gently—a week and a half before the dance—as they were leaving for their separate buses. "I'm allergic to your dog," he lied. "You always have dog hair all over you, and I'd be sneezing all night."

The creature's name was Muffin, or Cupcake, or Sweet Buns, or something like that, one of those yippy little hairball types. Denise was worse about that dog than the average mother was with her newborn, so she didn't take the news well at all. Worse yet, she didn't believe him.

Standing right out there on the steps of the school with all the buses filled or filling and the rest of the school pouring out around them, Denise had pointed at him and shrieked—shrieked!—to the world: "Four weeks ago Billy Essler promised to take me to the graduation dance, and now, after I've bought my dress and it's too late to go with anybody else, he's backing out because he's too cheap!"

Bill expected people to laugh at Denise for making a fool of herself, but, instead, they started booing at him—boys and girls alike. Seventh graders shot spitballs at him as their buses pulled out. Alex Morreale, star of the soccer team and named in the yearbook as Student Most People Would Like to Be, intentionally bumped him, practically knocking him over. Alex muttered, "Shabby, Essler," and the other kids took it up. "Shabby," they told him, one by one, as they passed, bumping.

"It's not my fault," he protested. "My family's too poor."

But he'd spent the last month bragging about the almost-four-hundred dollars he had in his own bank account, and every day at lunch he and the other guys had looked through computer catalogs, discussing which were the best games for him to buy. So for the whole bus ride home, people had stepped on his toes and "accidentally" smacked the back of his head with their backpacks.

Now, safely at home, Bill tried to forget his

problems by turning on his computer. He switched on the modem, accessed his service, then called up the Internet, trying to find something interesting enough to take his mind off the fact that he'd just become the most unpopular kid in school.

There was nothing going on at the usual places Bill went. Monday nights there was a computer games forum, where people discussed what was new or how to handle specific puzzles or challenges in the latest games, but that wouldn't start for hours.

Bill spent about twenty minutes just surfing or lurking—visiting teleconferences without saying anything—and was about to turn off the modem and switch to one of his games when—under the SERVICES menu—he scrolled past a listing that made him stop, think to himself, *Naw, I didn't really see that,* then back up a page.

CURSES, INC.

Bill was bored enough to be intrigued. He clicked on it.

The screen dissolved to midnight blue with sparkly stars. There was a faint sound effect—tiny crystal bells, Bill was sure, not that he'd ever heard tiny crystal bells. Then a message appeared:

WELCOME TO CURSES, INC.

The stars faded away. A new message appeared:

SERVICES AVAILABLE:

JINX   HEX

GEAS   BANE

MALEDICTION

Weird, Bill thought. Not being sure what some of the words meant, and uncertain what the difference was between others, Bill clicked on the little box marked *?* on the menu bar at the top of the screen.

The screen showed:

JINX

An ongoing spell of either limited or unlimited duration.

Examples of JINX spells:

    causing the subject to fall down the next five sets of stairs encountered;

    causing the subject to fall down all sets of stairs encountered for one week's time;

    causing the subject to fall down all sets of stairs encountered for the rest of the subject's life.

CLICK TO CONTINUE

HEX

A onetime spell that either may or may not be repeatable.

Examples of HEX spells:

    causing the subject to fall down the
       stairs one time;

    causing the subject to die.

CLICK TO CONTINUE

GEAS

A compulsion laid on someone.

Example of a GEAS spell:

    causing the subject to go up or down
       every set of stairs encountered.

CLICK TO CONTINUE

BANE

A changing of someone's nature.

Example of a BANE spell:

    causing the subject to believe he or
       she IS a set of stairs.

CLICK TO CONTINUE

MALEDICTION

A general type of ill-wishing.
Example of a MALEDICTION spell:
   causing bad things to happen to the
      subject while on stairs, such as
      trips, splinters, or arguments.

CLICK TO CONTINUE

Generally speaking, JINX spells are the most
expensive curses, MALEDICTION spells the
least.

RETURN TO PREVIOUS MENU

Bill paused to consider. *Expensive?* He'd thought this would just be something to print out, some sort of official-looking certificate: This is to inform you that you have been officially cursed.... That sort of thing. It was a wonderful idea. Maybe, he decided, these Curses, Inc. people were just trying to be cute. Or maybe they printed the certificates themselves, on fancy parchment, and the more printing that was required, the more they'd charge. It didn't make any difference; he could always cancel if it turned out there was an actual payment required. Meanwhile, he was having fun.

Bill clicked on RETURN TO PREVIOUS MENU.

SERVICES AVAILABLE:

JINX	HEX
GEAS	BANE
MALEDICTION	

Bill clicked JINX.

CURSES:

PLACING	REMOVING
MODIFYING	

After Denise had made such a fool of him? He clicked on PLACING.

DURATION OF JINX BY:

NUMBER OF OCCURRENCES
LENGTH OF TIME

Bill clicked on LENGTH OF TIME.

LENGTH OF TIME OF JINX:

SECONDS	MINUTES
HOURS	DAYS
WEEKS	MONTHS
YEARS	

```
TILL DEATH DO US PART
FOREVER
```

Bill figured FOREVER probably concerned haunting. The last thing he wanted was Denise hanging around forever. He clicked on TILL DEATH DO US PART.

```
JINXES INVOLVING:

BODY FUNCTIONS
CHARACTER
ABILITY
INTELLIGENCE
REACTIONS TO OTHER PEOPLE
REACTIONS BY OTHER PEOPLE
MISCELLANEOUS
```

How could anybody resist BODY FUNCTIONS?

```
JINXES INVOLVING BODY FUNCTIONS:

ERUPTIONS
DISCHARGES
HAIR GAINS/LOSSES
WEIGHT GAINS/LOSSES
BODY MEMBERS GAINS/LOSSES
LOSS OF CONTROL OF BODILY FUNCTIONS
GENERAL APPEARANCE
```

Bill chose ERUPTIONS.

TYPE OF ERUPTIONS:

ACNE	BOILS
HERPES	PSORIASIS
WARTS	

MISCELLANEOUS CONTAGIOUS RASHES

MISCELLANEOUS FATAL RASHES

WARTS, Bill decided, going for the traditional. *Definitely warts.*

WARTS:

CHRONIC   INTERMITTENT

Bill clicked on CHRONIC.

DENSITY:

1% - 100%

Bill moved the little arrow to 100%.

START DATE OF CURSE:

IMMEDIATELY

TYPE DATE/TIME HERE:

IMMEDIATELY, Bill clicked.

TYPE SUBJECT'S NAME HERE:

TYPE SUBJECT'S ADDRESS HERE:

Bill typed in DENISE BAINBRIDGE. He checked the phone book for her address and typed that in at the appropriate space.

INFORMATION SUFFICIENT FOR IDENTIFICATION.

CLICK ANYWHERE TO PROCEED.

Bill clicked.

You have ordered a

Till Death Do Us Part

JINX Curse

of chronic warts

to cover 100% of Denise Bainbridge's body.

CORRECT AS IS   CHANGES REQUIRED

CORRECT AS IS, Bill clicked.

Payment required before delivery of services

Amount due: $575

CASH

CREDIT CARD

SAVINGS/CHECKING ACCOUNT

Bill nearly choked, even considering that he assumed he'd missed a decimal point. He looked again and saw he hadn't.

He clicked on QUIT.

Perhaps you are not aware that CURSES, INC. guarantees 100% satisfaction, or a full refund cheerfully given.

Do you really want to quit?

YES   NO

These people were *definitely* weird. Bill clicked YES, half expecting... He shivered, not knowing what he expected.

Perhaps some other time ...

The words faded to the dark, starry sky, there was that faint tinkling that might be tiny crystal bells, then the screen returned to the Curses, Inc. icon in amongst all the other companies' icons.

Bill shook his head and shivered again. Some people had the weirdest sense of humor.

Bill had absolutely no intention of ever going back to Curses, Inc.

But the following day at school he got alternately ignored, razzed, and physically intimidated by what had to be at least three-quarters of the student population. And it was all Denise's fault. By the time he got home, he figured Curses, Inc. had to have *some*thing in his price range.

He turned on the modem, easily found Curses, Inc. once again, but this time, after the stars disappeared, the screen printed out:

MONEY A CONCERN?

YES   NO

They remembered him. And knew why he had quit yesterday. Spooky. Still, YES, Bill clicked.

PRICE RANGE:

JINX SPELLS:
$200–$500 $501–$1,000
$1,001 and up
(Most JINX spells are under $1,500)

HEX SPELLS:
BELOW $50 $51–$100
$101–$250 $251 and up
(Most HEX spells are affordably priced
under $500)

GEAS SPELLS—to be individually
negotiated
(starting at $500)

> BANE SPELLS—to be individually
> negotiated
> (starting at $500)

> MALEDICTION SPELLS—our most
> popular with children
> (starting at $5)

> CURSES, INC. guarantees 100% satisfaction,
> or a full refund cheerfully given.

Wow! Bill thought, never having realized how expensive curses could be. But he didn't like being called a child, and maledictions sounded too wimpy. He clicked on HEX SPELLS/BELOW $50.

MAY WE SUGGEST:

MINOR SCARES
PETTY ANNOYANCES
SPELLS AGAINST SUBJECT'S HOME
SPELLS AGAINST SUBJECT'S PETS/
LIVESTOCK

Happily, Bill paused to consider. Surely, he reasoned, a curse against a miserable mutt like Muffin had to be cheaper than a curse against a person. He clicked on SPELLS AGAINST SUBJECT'S PETS/ LIVESTOCK.

TYPE OF ANIMAL:

FARM   PET

EXOTIC

Bill clicked on PET.

IS SUBJECT'S PET:

BIRD   CAT

DOG   FISH

SMALL MAMMAL   WERE-CREATURE

OTHER

Bill clicked DOG, since Yappy Varmints Named after Small, Undigestible Pastries wasn't one of the options.

Curses to change the nature or appearance of subject's pet are slightly beyond the price limit you have set, leaving these options:

CAUSE DEATH   CAUSE LOSS

RETURN TO PRICE RANGE MENU

Much as Bill dearly loved the idea of changing Denise's dog so that either she or it thought it was something else, he decided that BELOW $50 was as high as he was going to go for this. In fact, he wanted to go as far BELOW $50 as possible. He clicked on CAUSE DEATH.

Range: $40–$50, depending on manner of death.

CONTINUE

RETURN TO PREVIOUS PAGE

Bill shook his head and clicked on RETURN TO PREVIOUS PAGE.

Curses to change the nature or appearance of subject's pet are slightly beyond the price limit you have set, leaving these options:

CAUSE DEATH   CAUSE LOSS

RETURN TO PRICE RANGE MENU

This time Bill clicked on CAUSE LOSS.

Permanent loss is beyond the price range you have set, leaving these options:

TEMPORARY LOSS

RETURN TO PRICE RANGE MENU

TEMPORARY LOSS, Bill ordered.

START DATE OF CURSE:

IMMEDIATELY
TYPE DATE/TIME HERE:

IMMEDIATELY. Then once again the computer asked for the subject's name and address, and Bill typed that information in. The screen said:

You have ordered a
HEX Curse
of temporary loss
of Denise Bainbridge's pet dog,
effective immediately.

CORRECT AS IS   CHANGES REQUIRED

Bill clicked CORRECT AS IS.

Payment required before delivery of services
Amount due: $25
CASH
CREDIT CARD
SAVINGS/CHECKING ACCOUNT

Bill was too eager to get started to bother with sending cash, and he certainly didn't have a credit card. He clicked on SAVINGS/CHECKING ACCOUNT.

Mount Morris Community Savings Bank records one savings account in the name of
    William Franklin Essler,
    account number: 53-0057-995239,
    showing a current balance of $395.

                    Proceed?
        YES   NO

Bill sat back in amazement. These Curses, Inc.
people were good. Apparently they had traced
him by his parents' Internet account, then his personal password, and then found his savings account. It was kind of unsettling, knowing how
much people could find out about you. He clicked
on YES.

                Curse proceeding.

                Any further requests?
            YES   NO

Bill clicked on NO.

CURSES, INC. appreciates your patronage.

With that faint sound of bells, the message faded into the company's starry night background, which was in turn replaced by the Curses, Inc. icon.

Bill couldn't wait to get to school tomorrow.

When Bill walked into homeroom, he expected to see Denise all teary and sniffly, but she looked and sounded fine. In fact, she was talking animatedly, and she and her circle of friends were laughing.

People were still avoiding him except to give him dirty looks, so nobody seemed to care when he casually drifted across the room to look out the windows and ended up close enough to Denise's group to listen in.

"So I leave the deli," Denise was saying, "waving this one slice of baloney, and I'm going, 'Here, Muffin, sweetie. Mama has your favorite food,' and I'm passing by this Dumpster, and all of a sudden out jumps Muffin, and she lands on my shoulder, and I'm going like this"—Denise threw her hands up and mimed being startled—"and the little monster knows the baloney's for her, and she just sits there on my shoulder and starts eating like she thinks she's a parrot or something."

The girls laughed that oh-isn't-that-*cute* laugh girls do.

"So all in all she was only gone fifteen minutes,"

Denise finished just as the bell for first period sounded. Turning and seeing Bill, she snarled, "Move, jerk," even though she could have just as easily walked around him.

"Move, jerk," other girls and a few of the boys said, knocking into him, so that—eventually—he dropped his books, and everybody walked right over them.

Bill hardly noticed. *Fifteen minutes?* he thought. *I paid twenty-five dollars to have that stupid little mutt missing for fifteen minutes?*

Wait until he got home and told Curses, Inc. what he thought of that.

Determined to demand his twenty-five dollars returned, Bill was hoping for an address or phone number when he clicked on MORE INFO on the menu bar.

But before he had a chance to do that, as soon as he clicked on the Curses, Inc. icon but after he heard the tiny chiming of the bells and saw the WELCOME TO CURSES, INC. message, instead of listing the SERVICES AVAILABLE, the screen showed:

WELCOME BACK TO CURSES, INC.,
VALUED CUSTOMER, WILLIAM FRANKLIN ESSLER.

WOULD YOU LIKE TO:

INQUIRE INTO STATUS OF PREVIOUS
        PURCHASE?
MAKE A COMPLAINT?
OPEN A NEW MATTER?

Hah! Bill thought. If fifteen minutes for twenty-five dollars was the best they could do, no wonder they offered MAKE A COMPLAINT on their menu. He clicked on that.

Our records show one transaction, placed yesterday at 3:37 P.M. (Eastern Daylight Saving Time), at which time you ordered one HEX Curse to be placed on Denise Bainbridge to result in temporary loss of a pet dog.

Our records further indicate curse was completed at 3:42 P.M. (EDST) and took effect at 4:17 P.M. of the same day, at which time the animal in question ran out a door opened by curse subject's mother returning home from work.

Our records also indicate payment of $25 debited from your savings account 53-0057-995239 at Mount Morris Community Savings Bank upon successful placement of curse.

FURTHER INQUIRY
RETURN TO PREVIOUS PAGE

Bill clicked on FURTHER INQUIRY.

PLEASE HOLD

Bill held for about a minute, at which point the message dissolved, with the tinkling of those stupid bells, into the starry night screen. For an instant he thought Curses, Inc. had broken the connection, but then a message started, letter by letter, and Bill realized he'd reached a real person rather than an automatic program.

Greetings. This is Edanna.
How may I assist you?

Bill typed in: "The dog was gone for fifteen lousy minutes. I want my money back."

I'm sorry, sir. You purchased a TEMPORARY Loss of Pet Curse.

"Fifteen minutes is VERY temporary," Bill typed.

> I'm sorry you're dissatisfied, sir. However, the spell was delivered as ordered. If you had wanted to stipulate a spell of longer duration, you should have said so. Under the circumstances, I'm afraid we are unable to refund your purchase price.

"One hundred percent satisfaction guaranteed," Bill muttered to himself. He typed, "You never asked how long I wanted the spell to last."

> Sir, a $25 Temporary Loss of Pet Curse is assigned a random duration from 1 minute to 24 hours.

This was getting nowhere. Bill realized they would never refund his twenty-five dollars. Instead of worrying about that, he typed: "How much to assign a particular amount of time?"

> $30, sir.

Bill sighed. The twenty-five dollars was gone; did he want to throw another thirty dollars after that? Bill sighed again. The twenty-five dollars was gone with nothing to show for it. He typed: "OK. But I want the dog gone for at least two weeks." That would be until after the dance, and it would serve Denise right.

I'm sorry, sir. Perhaps I didn't make myself clear. $30 would guarantee the dog being missing for whatever amount of time you stipulated LESS THAN 24 hours. Two weeks would cost $170.

Bill gave a groan that was half growl.

But twenty-four hours was such a piddling little amount.

"How much," he typed, "for two days?" That would be over the weekend, giving Denise all that free time on her hands to worry.

---

48 hours would cost $40, sir.

It seemed foolish to pay thirty dollars, then cheap out at the last minute and lose a whole extra day for ten dollars. He *had* the money. "OK," he typed, reluctantly.

Let me switch you over to our regular program, sir. I'd like to add, sir, that it's been a pleasure doing business with you.

Edanna

Her name was followed by a symbol of a smiley face wearing a stylized pointed witch's hat. A moment later the screen dissolved to show:

You have ordered a
HEX Curse
of temporary (48-hour)
loss of Denise Bainbridge's pet dog,
effective immediately.

CORRECT AS IS　　　　　CHANGES REQUIRED

Bill clicked on CORRECT AS IS and finished up with the business of letting Curses, Inc. deduct the money from his savings account. It was only when he was back to the main menu that he realized he should have had the curse start tomorrow morning—Saturday—so that the dog would still be missing when Denise got to school Monday. That way, unless her parents called the office to let her know it had been found, it would have been like getting almost a full day free.

Dummy, Bill chided himself.

Still, all in all he was well pleased.

Bill spent the weekend gleefully drawing mental pictures of a dismayed Denise Bainbridge wandering the streets of Mount Morris with an increasingly fossilized-looking slice of baloney, calling, "Come to Mama, Muffin."

On Monday he got to school right after her. As he walked down the hall behind her, he heard her tell a group of girls, "You will never *believe* what happened to me this weekend."

Which was a good start, except that she sounded excited, not distressed.

"First of all," Denise started, "remember how my aunt picked me up from school Friday to spend the weekend at her cottage on the lake?"

Picked her up from school? Bill's mind echoed hollowly. *To spend the weekend...* His steps faltered. He had to make a conscious effort not to turn to the nearest locker and bang his head on it. *I spent forty dollars to have that idiot dog lost for the weekend, and Denise wasn't even home to miss it?*

He realized that the girls were getting away from him and he hurried to catch up to hear the rest of it.

"It was *such* fun," Denise was saying. "I've got to tell you all about it later. But *first* let me tell you what happened when I got back Sunday afternoon. I walk into the living room—right?—and there, sitting on the couch with my mom and dad, is this extremely *gorgeous* guy with this *wonderful* dark hair and brown eyes—let me tell you—to die for. And he's our age—right?—but he stands up when I walk into the room—he actually *stands up*. And he says in this rich, sexy Spanish accent, 'Ah! This must be Denise.' "

The girls all gave appreciative sighs and moans and asked who he was.

"His name is Rafael, and he's somehow related to the *Spanish royal family,* and he's an exchange student who's going to be spending the entire next year with the family whose backyard is up against ours."

The girls started to chatter excitedly, and Denise had to talk over them, "But listen to this—do you want to hear the best part? The reason he came over was that *Muffin* got loose again while I was away, and Rafael *found* her. He's *crazy* about dogs especially now because he had to leave his back home in Spain and he's missing them. He asked me"—Denise rested her hand over her heart and said, in her attempt at a sexy accent—" 'Would it be permitted, Denise, for me to occasionally come to visit with your dog?' And then he looks at me with those *incredible* eyes and asks, 'Would it be permitted to visit you, too?' "

What have I done? Bill thought, unable to follow them any further, to listen to any more. *Thanks to my forty dollars, Denise doesn't get a chance to worry about her dog, but she gets to meet Señor Prince Charming.*

Something had to be done.

Bill got home and once again told the computer he needed MAKE A COMPLAINT. Once again he got Edanna on the line, she of the witch-hatted smiley face. "Denise met some sort of Spanish count or something," Bill complained.

Edanna replied:

I'm sorry, sir. You never indicated a particular way for the curse subject's dog to be returned. And, because it was a temporary spell, the dog HAD to be returned.

"Yeah, yeah," Bill muttered as he typed. "But she came out better than she started." But even as he typed it, he knew what the answer would be:

I really don't see how we can give you a refund when none of this was covered by the terms of our agreement, sir.

Would you like to buy an additional spell for the dog to be lost for another 48 hours and then return on its own?

Bill typed, "Can I afford it?"

Ensuring that the dog would return on its own requires a JINX Temporary Change Animal's Nature spell, an additional $90, for a total charge of $130.

Ouch, Bill thought. He typed, "Forget the dog. Any cheaper suggestions?"

Minor Scares, such as narrowly avoiding a fatal mishap.

Petty Annoyances, making any of a variety of things go wrong.

Spells against Subject's Home, perhaps causing breakage.

Bill decided that Minor Scares would be over too quickly, and Spells against Subject's Home seemed more against Denise's parents. He typed, "Tell me more about Petty Annoyances." At the last second, before hitting RETURN, he added, "As cheap as possible."

$5 Spells:

— Neighbor's Gate Swings Shut with a
   Loud Bang in the Middle of the Night
— Subject Steps on Gum That Sticks to
   Shoe
— Pencil Point Breaks

More examples?

Those were a bit *too* petty, just a moment's annoyance. "How about $10 spells?" Bill asked.

—Sandwich Falls Peanut-Butter Side Down
—Grass Stains Get on White Sneakers
—Panty Hose Runs

More?

Bill took a deep breath. "Could I get something with longer-lasting effects for $25?" he typed.

—Lost Homework
—Forgotten Orthodontist Appointment
—Incorrectly Set VCR Resulting in
  Missed Program

More?

Bill didn't like any of those, but thinking about homework gave him an idea. After all, it was in school, in front of everyone, that Denise had humiliated him. "How about she drops her tray at lunch, everything falls off, and everybody laughs at her?"

$35 for tray to drop
$ 5 to ensure everything falls off

+ $475 for everyone to laugh
$515 total for spell

Acceptable?

"NO!" Bill typed before Edanna finished the word *Acceptable?* He thought about school some more. Time was short. This was the last full week. In fact, exams started tomorrow. He got a wonderful idea. "How much to make her fail an exam?" he typed.

To make her fail in her weakest subject:
$60
To make her fail in her strongest subject:
$217

Bill ran his hands through his hair. *Sixty dollars!* But it was a good one.

"What's her weakest subject?" he typed, worried—the way things were going—it would turn out to be something inconsequential, like art, and he'd have to pay more for a required subject.

The answer came back:

Math.

He typed, "OK. Make her fail in math." He rested his head on the desk while he and Curses,

Inc. went through the process of deducting sixty dollars from his dwindling account.

During Tuesday's math exam, Bill glanced over to watch Denise so often that Mrs. McGuire warned, "Eyes on your own paper, Mr. Essler."

But Denise was having a hard time—Bill could tell by all the sighs, and by the way she kept running her hand through her hair.

When will she find out? he wondered, delighted at how he'd spent his latest investment.

The delight lasted until Thursday morning.

"Mrs. McGuire called my house last night to say I flunked my math exam," Bill heard Denise tell her friends, and he knew he was in trouble by the way she said it.

Not nearly upset enough, he thought with foreboding, though the girls made dismayed-sounding noises.

"Sixty-four," Denise said. "I flunked by one stupid little point—can you believe it? Luckily my average for the year was eighty-one, so I still pass the course, but, boy, were my parents mad." Denise flashed a smile. "But I was lucky again. Rafael"— Bill hated the smug singsong way she said that name—"was visiting when it happened, and guess *what?* It turns out he's a *math genius.* He's here on a *math scholarship.*" She'd saved the best for last and squealed, all in one breath, "And he said he'd tutor me in math over the summer."

The girls began jumping up and down the way excited girls do.

But then it turned out that *hadn't* been the best. Denise said, "And he said he'd take me to the dance tomorrow night! Mrs. McGuire said it'd be OK, since *someone*"—everyone turned to glare at Bill— "stood me up at the last minute after I bought my dress and everything."

Bill ignored her self-satisfied smile. In fact, he gave one of his own. He knew exactly what to do.

WELCOME BACK TO CURSES, INC.,
VALUED CUSTOMER, WILLIAM FRANKLIN
ESSLER.
WOULD YOU LIKE TO:

INQUIRE INTO STATUS OF PREVIOUS
PURCHASE?
MAKE A COMPLAINT?
OPEN A NEW MATTER?

Bill knew how far he'd get with MAKE A COM-PLAINT. He clicked on OPEN A NEW MATTER.

He kept on clicking until he got to PETTY AN-NOYANCES.

CATEGORIES OF ANNOYANCES:

NOISES   ODORS

ANIMALS   CHILDREN

FAMILY   OTHER PEOPLE

MOTOR VEHICLES   PERSONAL
                              POSSESSIONS

WEATHER   BODY FUNCTIONS

PLANTS/VEGETATION   OTHER

PERSONAL POSSESSIONS, Bill clicked.

CATEGORIES OF PERSONAL POSSESSIONS:

FOOD

CLOTHING

DWELLING

OBJECTS WITHIN DWELLING

MEANS OF TRANSPORTATION

OTHER

Bill chuckled to himself. *Oh,* CLOTHING, he thought, clicking on that one. *Definitely clothing.*

TYPES OF GARMENT:

UNDERGARMENTS	OUTERWEAR
SHIRT/BLOUSE	PANTS
SKIRT	DRESS
NIGHT APPAREL	ACCESSORIES

"The famous dress," Bill muttered, clicking on DRESS, "that we've all heard so much about for so long."

TYPE IDENTIFYING DESCRIPTION OF GARMENT:

Bill typed, "Denise Bainbridge's dress that she bought for the eighth-grade dance."

INFORMATION SUFFICIENT FOR
IDENTIFICATION

NATURE OF ANNOYANCE:

FIT	STATIC
STAIN	RIP

Bill clicked on RIP.

EXTENT OF DAMAGE:

PINPRICK - - - - - - - - - CAN'T BE WORN IN
HOLE   POLITE SOCIETY

Bill moved the little arrow to CAN'T BE WORN IN POLITE SOCIETY.

START DATE OF CURSE:

IMMEDIATELY
TYPE DATE/TIME HERE:

Bill typed, "Tomorrow, just as Denise is about to enter the dance."

That'll fix her, he thought. *Her and her miniature earl.*

He hesitated only once, when the price came up at eighty-five dollars. That would leave him—after his wonderful $395 that he had started with just last week—$185.

That would be enough to buy the two computer games he'd most wanted—though he'd started with a list of eight. Or, if he could make Mom feel guilty enough about his missing the dance because of her and she gave him ten dollars, he could buy the desktop publishing program he'd been looking at. With that, he could probably earn enough money to buy a couple games by the end of summer.

It was worth it, he decided, giving Curses, Inc. the go-ahead. There was no way Denise could come out on top with a ruined dress at the very last instant.

All day Friday Bill enjoyed himself because he knew that while he was the only person in the Thomas Jefferson eighth-grade class not planning to go to the dance, there was someone else who wasn't going to make it.

He went to sleep that night thinking how miserable Denise was at that very moment.

Saturday, when he came down for breakfast, his father said, "Hey, isn't this your girlfriend's picture in the paper?"

"I don't have a girlfriend," Bill said, but he glanced over anyway.

The picture was labeled: RAGS TO RABBITS. And there was Denise, wearing a T-shirt and jeans, and somebody who had to be her Spanish duke—wearing a tuxedo, of all things. The two of them were grinning and holding between them what had to be the hugest stuffed rabbit Bill had ever seen, about the size of a chubby seven-year-old.

"What?" Bill yelped, snatching the paper from his father.

The article explained that Denise Bainbridge and her date Rafael-with-three-or-four-last-names-that-Bill-didn't-bother-trying-to-decipher were going to an eighth-grade graduation dance. Getting out of the limousine that Rafael had hired (apparently the guy really *was* rich), Denise had caught her dress on the door handle, ripping the skirt section half off from the top.

"I was all upset," the paper quoted Denise as saying, "and I had nothing else appropriate to wear, so
Rafael suggested we skip the dance and go to the
fair instead."

Once there, the paper went on, Rafael—who described himself as an expert marksman—had gone
to the firing range, winning prizes that he kept trading up, till they ended with the amazing twenty-
five-pound rabbit. When the fair manager came out
to congratulate Denise and Rafael, they told him
how they had come to be there, and the manager
felt so sorry for Denise's disastrous date that he
called the office at Thomas Jefferson and told prin-
cipal Sol Washburn to announce that "any of
Denise's friends who wanted to come to the fair after the dance would get unlimited free rides."

There was a second picture, which Bill hadn't
even noticed before, with a bunch of his classmates
mugging for the camera.

He crumpled the page, despite his father's startled "Hey!" and walked very slowly back up to his
room, where he turned on the computer.

Once again it was Edanna who came on-line
when Bill indicated he needed to speak to someone
directly. Perhaps she was the only employee—perhaps she *was* Curses, Inc. Bill was so upset he kept
hitting two or three keys at once.

"I WANT HER AS MISERABLE AS I AM," Bill
typed in all capitals to indicate he was shouting.

"SHE'S MADE ME USE UP MOST OF MY MONEY AND RUINED MY SUMMER. I WANT TO RUIN HER SUMMER, TOO."

Edanna, as always, remained calm.

I'm sorry, sir, a Ruined Summer Curse is one of our most expensive MALEDICTION curses and would cost $475.

How about an Unhappiest Day Curse?

"You mean," Bill typed, still fumbling with the keys, "I can name one day that would be the unhappiest day of her life?"

Well, I'm afraid an Unhappiest Day of Her LIFE Curse would cost considerably more than you have at the moment, sir. But we could guarantee your presence on the unhappiest day of her SUMMER.

"How much?" Bill typed.

Normally, the cost for an Unhappiest Day Curse for an entire season would be $200.

Checking our records, I see the balance of your savings account is $185. Since you're such a valued customer of long standing,

I'm willing to bend the rules just a
little.

Bill had learned to be suspicious in his dealings with Curses, Inc. He typed, "But it'll still be her unhappiest day? You aren't going to make it her second most unhappiest day?"

No, sir, of course not. It will be our
standard Unhappiest Day Curse, just offered
at a slight discount, because it's you.

Bill got an unaccountably sentimental feeling at the thought that he'd become someone special to Edanna, that she was trying to look out for him. "Thank you," he typed. He shut his eyes, trying to block out the picture of the balance of his savings account going down to all zeros. "Do it."

The day Bill scheduled to be the unhappiest day of Denise's summer was that Monday, the last day of school. There were no classes; it was a field day: They spent about half an hour cleaning out their desks and lockers, got their report cards, then the rest of the time was just a bunch of running around and games.

Even under normal circumstances, Bill hated field days, but this one was worse than usual because nobody was talking to him. *Every*body was talking to Denise. She was still the big hero for getting everybody those free fair passes. All the while he kept waiting for something to go wrong for her: for somebody to kick the ball so that it hit her in the mouth and broke her front teeth, for her to get her arm pulled out of its socket during tug-of-war, for her to get into an argument with her best friend.

None of that happened. Denise won every game she played, so that all the kids were continually begging for her to join their team, be their lucky player. She was laughing and being the center of attention and having a great time.

Maybe she'll get run over by the bus, Bill thought hopefully as the day finally ended.

But Denise didn't go home by bus that day.

Rafael, riding a bicycle built for two, came to pick her up.

Even if she DIES today, Bill thought all the long, lonely bus ride to his house, *it's still been a good day for her.*

Furious, he turned on the computer and clicked on the Curses, Inc. icon. There was no way they could refuse his money back after this.

The familiar blue background with stars came on, accompanied by the tinkling of those infuriating bells.

WELCOME TO CURSES, INC.,
BILL ESSLER.
AND HOW WAS *YOUR* DAY?

This screen faded away without waiting for a response, which was a good thing, for Bill was too furious to respond coherently. Words appeared on the screen and slowly scrolled upward.

I imagine you have some questions, and I imagine I know exactly what they are, so here's some answers without your even having to ask.

The answer to your first question is:

Yes, this WAS the unhappiest day of Denise's summer.

Tomorrow she will get a call from a reporter on the local TV news, who saw her picture in the paper. They'll do a feature on her and find her so photogenic and so congenial that . . .

...the day after, they will call her and ask her to do a daily five-minute segment on teen news. Then...

...the following day, Denise will get a call from a department store fashion coordinator who has seen her on television and who wants her to model clothes for their fall catalog, which is being photographed even now, so that...

...the very next day they'll fly her to Hawaii for location shots, where she'll be introduced to a Hollywood director who's...

Well, I'm sure you get the picture, Bill. Denise is going to have a very exciting and wonderful summer, and she's going to love every minute of it, so that's why today was the worst day of her summer.

As for your second question, the answer is:

Yes, I have to admit I knew all this yesterday, but you never asked.

And the answer to your third question is:

Because Denise took out a Lose All Your
Money Curse on you before you ever con-
tacted us. First come/first served, you know.

A bit of free advice, Bill:

You really ought to learn to loosen up a bit.

After all that scrolled away, the smiley face with
the witch's hat appeared, and the message:

Don't call us, we'll call you. . . .

Then that faded away, slowly.

And when Bill frantically looked for the Curses,
Inc. icon, that was gone, too.

Skin Deep

ARDDA LIVED IN A COTTAGE in the woods a half day's journey from the village. This arrangement suited Ardda for two reasons. One was because this way she didn't have people hounding her day and night with spur-of-the-moment requests for frivolous wishes: Let me win at cards (a request that frequently came from several people simultaneously); I need a breeze so my laundry will dry faster; we need less breeze for our picnic; make my cake rise; mend my cracked pot; and on and on. . . . By making people travel half a day to her cottage and half a day back home, Ardda knew that they had at least spent some time thinking about whatever they were asking for.

There was a more important reason why Ardda lived away from the village, however. Though she was sixteen years old, and though she had memories going as far back as when she had been about two years old, she couldn't remember a day when some villager hadn't said—or whispered—"What an ugly girl."

For Ardda had eyes that were narrow and squinty, a nose that was too big, and hair that was a muddy brown color and hung perfectly straight and limp so that—no matter how clean it was and how she'd fussed with it—she always looked as though someone had just dumped a pail of dirty water over her head.

All of this was nothing. The first thing anybody noticed about Ardda was the purple-colored birthmark that covered half her left cheek. Children were always coming up to her, pointing, and demanding in an accusing voice, "What's *that*?" Or strangers passing through the village would ask if she'd been burned when she was a baby. Or people would pat her on the head and murmur, "Poor thing."

Often, during Ardda's growing-up years, she would hear the adults whisper to one another, "Such a pity. And she's such a sweet-natured and kind thing." But the young people Ardda's own age were less sympathetic and much, much crueler. No amount of generosity or helpfulness would win them over. They had only stopped openly tormenting her when it became obvious—sometime around her twelfth summer—that she had the ability to change things with her wishes.

One of the things she changed—of course—was the way she looked. She couldn't make a permanent change; in fact, it wasn't even a real change, it was only a glamour: When she leaned over the wash-basin in the mornings, she could still see reflected in it the awful purple mark that covered so much of her face and the nose that seemed to cover most of what was left. But she could make other people think they saw a smooth pink cheek, a discreet little nose. She made them see—she wasn't greedy—not luxurious curls, but hair that didn't lie exactly flat against her forehead and down the sides of her face.

But the people knew what she really looked like. She heard them laugh. She heard them mutter, "Who does she think she's fooling?"

She considered a much stronger wish: She considered making them all forget she'd ever been any different than she appeared now.

But then she worried. Should she make her parents and brothers and sisters forget, too? And if they couldn't remember protecting her from the younger children's taunts, how much of her growing-up years would she have to erase from their minds? Should she make everyone believe she'd always been beautiful and they'd always loved her?

In the end she simply let go of the glamour, and—as soon as she was old enough to be on her own—she moved to the cottage in the woods.

That was how Ardda came to be alone one December afternoon of the year she was sixteen. As the snow began to fall thick and fast and Ardda was indoors safe and warm and comfortable, with a fire in the fireplace, a wool shawl around her shoulders, a purring cat on her lap, and a cup of tea in her hand, she heard a thumping sound from outside.

Somebody, she thought—or actually two or three somebodies from the amount of noise—was on her porch. What could have caused anyone to set out in such weather?

Ardda tried to shoo the cat off her lap. But the cat was lazy and comfortable and pretended not to understand, and it clung on to Ardda's skirt so that Ardda had to stand up to prove to the cat that she was serious about wanting it off.

And in all this while, Ardda realized, no one had knocked at the door, but the thumping from the porch continued.

Ardda opened the door and found herself face-to-face with a horse.

"Well, hello," Ardda said, grabbing the horse's bridle because the creature seemed ready to walk right in and make itself at home. "Aren't you a fine fellow? How kind of you to visit, but I'm afraid you can't come in."

The horse shook himself, making the tiny gold bells on his bridle jingle. He had obviously, Ardda thought, run long and hard through the woods. Despite the cold, he was lathered, and he had fresh scratches from bolting through the close-set trees.

"Do you have a master?" Ardda asked. "I see you must."

The horse was a magnificent stallion: big and well cared for—despite the scratches—and beautiful. The reins, the saddle, the decorative trappings all were made of the finest materials and must have cost a fortune.

"Did you leave your master behind?" Ardda asked, thinking maybe something in the woods had startled the horse, causing him to rear and throw his rider. But then Ardda saw that there was blood on the saddle and the reins and on the horse's neck and mane. Not the horse's blood, she surmised, not from the scratches, but as though someone had been injured, and had clung on for as long as possible before falling off.

Ardda forced the horse to bend his neck, to place his head against hers. "Tell me," she whispered, wishing for her mind to open to images from the horse's mind. The horse pictured himself walking through Ardda's open front door into a nice warm stable, fresh straw, fragrant hay, with Ardda herself—the horse fervently hoped—standing there holding a plump, juicy apple.

"Tell me," Ardda repeated, picturing in her own mind the woods, someone's arms around the horse's neck, the horse running.

The horse thought those were scary thoughts. He wanted to think about that warm stable.

Ardda pictured in her mind the small barn that was up against the back of the cottage. She pictured the goats she kept, and the chickens. She pictured herself leading the horse there, and rubbing him down, and giving him an apple. Then she pictured, again, the woods, and running, and the hurt rider.

She got a jumble of pictures: an enormous stable with stall after stall of other horses, a kind two-legs-who-provides-oats, who must be the owner. The horse wasn't clear on faces, but he recognized hands—and the owner had gentle hands, and apples often hidden in pockets. Then the horse was remembering riding through the woods, enjoying the crisp air, the running for the pure joy of running.

And then it got darker, and much colder, and the cold-white-little-things-that-sometimes-melt-and-sometimes-form-a-cold-blanket-on-the-ground started falling, and the two-legs faced him toward home—which the horse pictured as the stable. But other two-legs jumped out of the shadows of the trees and threw sticks-that-fly-and-are-sharp at them.

The horse—with a certain amount of self-satisfaction—pictured himself carrying his two-legs away to safety. But the two-legs was making hurt-sounding noises and leaking red-stuff-that-belongs-inside outside. The horse gave Ardda the image of the two-legs sliding off and falling into a pile of the cold-white-little-things-after-they-haven't-melted-but-have-formed-a-cold-blanket-on-the-ground.

"Good boy," Ardda told the horse. "You *are* a brave fellow to have gotten away from those bandits." She led him into the barn, rubbed the lather off his back and legs, and threw a blanket over him. It was too soon, after all that running, for him to eat, but she rested her forehead against his and sent him a picture of her presenting him with a whole armful of apples as soon as she came back.

She stopped back in the cottage itself just long enough to gather her cloak, a knife, a small clay cook pot, and some healing herbs.

Then she set out, following the horse's hoofprints in the snow, and hoped that she would find the injured man before he bled to death from the arrow wounds and before the snow covered up the horse's tracks.

With her cloak wrapped around her and her head down against the wind, Ardda came to a point where—between the failing light and the falling snow—she could no longer make out the horse's hoofprints.

She continued walking in the direction from which the horse seemed to have come.

The snow, though getting deeper by the

moment, was not yet deep enough to cover a man lying on the ground, even a man not moving. Periodically she called out into the absolute still-ness, "Hello? Hello?" But the snow seemed to eat up all sound, so that she couldn't be sure how close she'd need to be for anyone to hear her—if there was anyone alive to hear her.

All the while she walked, she wished fervently for the snow to stop. But this was a full-blown storm, much slower to turn away or kill in its tracks than some simple picnic-ruining breeze. The storm wouldn't end for hours, and she realized there was no way she could make it back home tonight.

She came to a lean-to, one of several the villagers used when collecting wood every spring and au-tumn. There'd be no wood now, but it would pro-vide some shelter. She would just go a little beyond, she determined, and then she must give up the search.

It was just as she was turning back that she no-ticed a lump up ahead. She had seen several lumps, which had all ended up being tree stumps or piles of wind-driven leaves or snowdrifts, and she told herself no, she'd gone far enough, she'd said she'd stop here. But then she told herself how awful she'd feel if she'd come so close only to give up seconds before finding the horse's lost rider. Sure she'd find nothing, she made her way to the lump.

And found the missing man.

He was still breathing—barely—and he had an arrow shaft sticking out of his shoulder, perilously close to his heart.

A prince, Ardda thought at the sight of his fine clothes and the gold and jewels he wore. *Or a very, very wealthy merchant.*

But there aren't merchants that wealthy, Ardda decided, *even in the port cities. Definitely a prince.*

A dying one.

Ardda weighed the necessity of getting him warm against the necessity of tending the wound.

In the end, she laid her hands against the injured shoulder, wished for his health and well-being with all her might, then she took hold of his feet and dragged him along the snowy path, using as much care as she could spare not to bang his head against rocks or tree stumps.

At the lean-to—three walls and a roof made of woven branches—she found broken-off sticks and twigs too small for the wood-gathering expedition to have bothered collecting, and she hastily arranged them into a pile. *"Fire,"* she wished, imagining the warmth of it on her outstretched fingers, seeing in her mind's eye a tiny flame catching, hearing it crackle, smelling the smoke.

Wishing worked best with a physical start. She wouldn't have had to wish nearly so hard if she'd taken the time to at least strike sparks with a flint, but she feared there wasn't time. She feared the young prince might die at any moment. Later on she might decide she'd been wrong, that she should have spent her wishing energy solely on healing; but there was no way to be sure.

Fire leapt from her fingertips, and already—after all her walking in the snowstorm—that little bit of wishing left her exhausted. She used up a few more precious seconds to nurse the fire, to set the clay pot over it, place a handful of snow and the herbs into the pot, and then she turned to the prince.

She wished strength into him, using up nearly all she had left herself to do so. Then she took her knife and cut the arrow out from his flesh. *"No bleeding,"* she wished, having nothing to spare for the pain.

The arrow came out, the prince didn't bleed to death, and Ardda packed the wound with the herbs, then wrapped it all with a length of fabric from her skirt since she hadn't thought to bring fresh cloths from home.

She spent the rest of the long night rubbing his limbs to keep him from losing them to the cold.

By midnight the snow stopped falling, and just after dawn—as she was blowing her breath onto his hands to warm his fingers—the prince opened his eyes.

Perhaps it was her face—or perhaps it was the young man's pain, or the smoke from the fire, or the first dazzling shaft of sunlight through the bare branches—but the prince winced, then kept his eyes closed.

"You will survive," Ardda told him, wish and comfort wrapped together. *"You will be fine."*

The prince nodded but didn't open his eyes.

He's weak from loss of blood, Ardda thought, and indeed in another moment she could tell by his breathing that he'd fallen back asleep.

But his reaction still hurt.

During the night she'd been pulling the lean-to apart branch by branch to keep the fire alive, but any more of that and the whole thing was likely to fall in on their heads. She changed the prince's bandage, and when that didn't wake him up, she dared to crawl out of the lean-to in search of what wood she could find in the vicinity. This she stacked in a pile close at hand.

He would not survive another night outdoors, she knew. He needed more warmth than this simple fire provided; he needed shelter from the wind, and hot broth to give him strength. She regretted not having the horse; except, of course, the horse had been exhausted and would have balked at traveling through the snow and wind last night. Fighting him, she wouldn't have made it this far. And in any

case the prince was obviously in no state to
ride.

Thinking of the horse reminded Ardda of the animal's impression of the prince: kind, and gentle,
and generous. Not, of course, she told herself, that
she was as fond of apples as the horse was.

But as she sat looking at the prince, thinking
how handsome he was, she thought that maybe—
if he got a chance to know her before he saw what
she looked like—maybe his basic goodness would
help him disregard her appearance.

So that when he stirred again and his eyelids
fluttered once more, Ardda wished the glamour
back on herself: a smooth cheek, an easy-to-live-
with nose, and—not being greedy—hair that didn't
exactly curl but framed her face loosely.

The prince opened his eyes.

"Be strong," Ardda wished at him. *"Be well."*

His eyes didn't stay open any longer than last
time, but he gave a tight smile: acknowledgment
that he heard her, and understood, and was trying
to be brave.

Her heart melted.

"My name is Ardda," she told him. She clasped
his hand. "I have the power of wishes, and I am
wishing very hard for you to *Get better.*"

He gave her hand a slight squeeze. "Thank you,"
he whispered, little more than a movement of his
lips.

"I have to leave," she told him, "to get your horse, to bring you back to the safety of my cottage. I am wishing *Wild animals away from here.* I am wishing you *Health.*"

"Garn," he whispered, which made no sense till he added, "Prince of Imryn," proving Ardda had been right. He put his hand over his heart: a bow if he'd been standing and if he'd had the strength—courtly manners that set Ardda's heart beating faster.

"I'll be back by noon," she wished and promised.

Prince Garn's eyes fluttered open for an instant, too short a time for Ardda to know whether he'd seen her. But she liked to think he had, for he fell back asleep with a smile.

There was not nearly the wind that there had been the night before, and what there was blew at her back. Ardda got to her cottage in good time. Along the way she had tried to decide whether she should construct some sort of litter for the prince that the horse could pull through the snow, but in the end she thought that would take too long and that it was likely to get caught in the snow anyway. She brought a stool, to help Garn mount, fed the horse apples, promised him many more, then clambered onto his back. Then, riding as fast as she dared, she returned to the lean-to.

The fire was down to almost nothing, despite

the pile of sticks she had left where Prince Garn could reach them. But the prince was breathing easily, and there were no tracks but her own near him.

"Garn," she said, shaking him awake. "Prince Garn."

"Ardda," he whispered, surprising her that he had remembered. He reached out his hand and brushed her cheek.

Did he remember and wonder? Or was it just tenderness?

"You have to stand." Ardda wished so much strength into him that her own knees became wobbly.

But he stood. He leaned on her shoulder to climb onto the stool. He swayed slightly, and she didn't think he was going to make it. But he gathered himself and swung up onto the horse.

By then Ardda needed the stool herself. She climbed up behind Garn, putting her arms around him to hold on to the reins, though she realized that if he started to fall, there was little she could do.

From this position, there was no way to retrieve the stool—yet another reason, if she was counting, not to let the prince fall off: She'd never get him back on.

She gave the reins a little shake so the horse

would walk slowly and started back toward her cottage.

After three days of lying on a pallet in front of Ardda's fireplace—wrapped in all of Ardda's warm blankets so that Ardda herself had to wear her cloak to bed to keep from freezing, spoon-fed Ardda's soup, subjected to Ardda's wishes for well-being, kept clean and dry and safe from the cat—Prince Garn finally could stay awake longer than five minutes at a time.

After four days he was strong enough to sit up by himself.

After six days he could get up out of his make-shift bed.

After ten days he was ready to go home.

"Come with me," he invited Ardda.

She had just brought in an armful of wood. To keep the prince warm day and night, she had burned much more than she had made provision for, and she had been thinking that, eventually, she would have to go out into the woods for more.

He took her hand, which she had wiped on her apron but which was still gritty from the bark, and he kissed it.

She loved his royal manners.

Still, Ardda felt her cheeks get warm. Then she worried. Did they redden at the same rate, she wondered, her natural right cheek and the glamour-affected left?

They must have. Garn smiled at her and said, "My family will love you. You're beautiful, you saved my life, you're kind and sweet and beautiful."

That was two *beautiful*s, Ardda noticed, but didn't let it worry her.

"My father can grant you lands, so you'll be a noble lady, so we can marry. If you're willing," Garn added hastily. He brushed the backs of his fingers against her cheek.

Ardda couldn't help but flinch, knowing what the cheek really looked like.

"What?" Garn asked.

"I'm not beautiful," Ardda told him. She only meant that even with the purple mark covered and the nose looking smaller than it really was, her eyes were still squinty and her hair was muddy brown and straight.

But the prince said, "Of course you're beautiful. I thought that from the first moment I saw you, even before I knew how wonderful you were, even before I knew you were going to save my life." But he frowned, slightly, even as he said this, as though trying, *trying* to remember...

It was time.

"I'm not beautiful," Ardda repeated.

"You are," the prince protested, somewhat weakly, somewhat breathlessly.

"I have the power of wishes," she reminded him. "I have wished a glamour on myself so that you could look at me without wincing."

"Nonsense," Garn said. "I'd love you anyway."

Ardda released the glamour.

Garn winced and looked away.

Ardda waited for him to repeat that he loved her anyway.

And waited.

Ardda closed *her* eyes.

She said, "I'm the same person I was before. I can keep the glamour. No one else need know."

"*I* would know," the prince answered.

"Yes," Ardda said.

She could wish for him to love her, but that seemed as wrong as tampering with her family's memories.

In the end, he packed provisions for the trip and said no more of taking her with him.

Ardda had returned the glamour to her face so that he would look at her before he left, but still he would not. Sitting astride his tall horse in her front yard, he looked at his hands on the reins and said, "I couldn't live a lie. Truth is not in what appears to be, but in what really is."

Ardda couldn't argue with that. All she *could* have said was that sometimes truth has nothing to do with what you can see.

But she didn't say that. She said, instead, "You're absolutely right."

And she cast a glamour on him.

She made him look as though he had pointy ears with tufts of fur at the ends. She covered his face with warts and made his eyes orange.

"Good-bye," she said, waving.

Garn, of course, had no idea what he looked like. He smiled, still not looking directly at her, gave an elegant half-bow, and put his heels to his horse's sides. He'd have a surprise when he got back to court, a surprise that would last for a year, but only a year.

Ardda picked up her cat. "You know," she told the cat, "I've been foolish. Of course everyone in my own village knows what I really look like, but Prince Garn has reminded me that the world is a big place."

The cat said, "Meow," which Ardda took as the most sensible thing anyone had said to her in a long time.

And with that she packed her own provisions and set out, with the cat, the goats, and the chickens. And with big, bright eyes and golden hair that was all luxurious curls—because sometimes you just have to be a little bit greedy.

PAST SUNSET

THERE WAS A STREET in the village where I grew up that everyone knew not to travel down past sunset.

During daylight hours it was a perfectly fine and normal street. Housewives opened their shutters and strung clotheslines across the way so that fresh-smelling laundry hung to dry two and three and four stories above the cobblestones that the neighborhood grandfathers kept well swept. Merchants from the surrounding countryside set up stalls to sell fresh fruit and vegetables, live chickens and rabbits. While the sun was there to warm the stones, you could hear the *clop clop* of horses' hooves and the rumble of the wooden wheels of carts and carriages. You could hear the laughter of young boys playing their chasing games and the rhythmic counting of girls playing their games of skipping and hand clapping.

But as the sun began to set, the farmers hurried to take down their stalls and return to the safety of their country homes. The housewives pulled in their sheets and shirts and locked the shutters. Those who lived on other streets of the village found different routes on their way home, and parents didn't have to call their children in because the children knew not to linger outside.

For when the shadows blended into night's darkness, there was a lady you would see if you were foolish enough to look. Your first thought might be that she was pale and beautiful, standing there in a white gown that flowed in the evening breeze. Silently, she would beckon for you to come closer. You might be fooled by her sad face. But then you might remember that there wasn't necessarily a breeze that night. And then you might notice that she was much too pale, even for a fine lady. And if you looked at her eyes...

Never look at her eyes, the stern grandmothers in their black shawls warned us—for there was no looking away.

The children of the village would always reach an age—for us girls it was often when we were nine or ten; for the boys, usually earlier—when all our parents' and grandparents' and neighbors' warnings weren't enough; when, in fact, those warnings only served to stir curiosity—and stir it and stir it, until we had to see for ourselves what we had so long been warned about; when we would find a way—there was always a way—to locate ourselves in a room that overlooked the street; when we would crack open the shutters and alternately hope and dread that this would be one of the nights that the ghostly lady appeared.

Those nights that she *did* appear, she always found the cracked-open shutter—no matter how quiet the would-be observer had been, and no matter that we almost always knew enough not to have a candle in there with us to show a telltale sliver of light into the street.

But she always knew.

And if there was an open window, she would come and stand directly beneath it, and—always silently—she would motion for that child to come out in the street to join her.

We might have been curious, but we weren't stupid.

If we were especially daring or if we weren't fast enough, the lady—whose feet normally seemed as firmly placed on the ground as our own—would begin to drift up, up, closer and closer until we would slam the shutters closed and stand or crouch with our hearts beating wildly, having seen that everything was exactly as it had always been described to us, and thankful that—for whatever reason—

this particular ghost's domain was outside, on our street, and she couldn't pass through walls or shutters.

But there was always the fear that someday a child would be too daring, or too slow.

This had never happened in recent memory. But Grand-mère Edmée—who wasn't actually any-body's grandmother, but who was probably the old-est person living in the village—Grand-mère Edmée remembered a ghost long before the citizens had risen up in revolution and sent the king and his family to the guillotine. Grand-mère Edmée said there had been a ghost when she herself was our age—a hard-enough concept to believe in itself—but she added that then the ghost was a young man, not a young woman. She also said that her own grandmother talked of a ghost who was an old woman—an old woman who had been cursed by a witch. But who she was or why she had been cursed, nobody knew. This talk of ghosts who changed age and gender made *us* say that Grand-mère Edmée had spent too much time in the wine cellar. But nobody wanted to see what would hap-pen if the ghost *did* touch you, or if you looked into her eyes.

All of this—all of it—changed the autumn I was twelve.

By then I had seen the ghostly lady often enough that I was cautious—no one ever outgrew caution—but I was no longer impressed. I would have gladly given up our famous ghost to live on a normal street, like my friends who could stay out past sunset and who could leave their windows open on a hot summer's night. As my brother Antoine had done before me, I became less interested in seeing the ghost and more interested in making sure the younger members of my family took no reckless chances.

In our house, where the kitchen and the parlor looked out over the street, the adults generally spent the evening in the parlor, with the shutters closed. We were two stories up, with the pâtisserie selling its wonderful tarts and pies on the ground floor and the Guignard family occupying the middle floor.

One evening of the year I was twelve, when autumn teetered on the brink of winter, I was in the kitchen, because my ten-year-old sister Mignon claimed to have a chill; this required sitting by the kitchen fire after the rest of the family had moved to the parlor. Our brother Gaetan, who was nine, had offered to keep her company—a clear signal, so far as I was concerned, that the kitchen shutters would bear close watching that night.

So I was embroidering a rose on a dinner napkin to cover a stain, while Gaetan whittled a piece of wood that was supposed to eventually be an extra sheep for the Christmas crèche, and Mignon—

sulking at being found out—was huddled close to the fire, wrapped in a blanket.

A noise at the side window made us all jerk our heads up.

It sounded like pebbles—or beans—hitting the outside of the shutters.

"Marianne," Mignon called to me in a whisper. "What was that?"

Before I could answer that I didn't know, a voice called, "Jules," which was my grandfather's name.

The voice belonged to the Widow Morin, who lived next door above the butcher's shop, her kitchen window separated from ours by a very narrow alley.

Mignon, in a strong voice that belied her claims of not feeling well, called out, "Grand-père! Maman! Papa!"

Fifteen-year-old Antoine was the first into the kitchen, followed by Maman, then Honorée—who was six—then Grand-père. Papa was last because he'd hurt his foot in an accident at the mill and he still had to use a cane.

"Jules!" the Widow Morin called. "Are you there? I need help."

"Open the window," Grand-père commanded us.

"No!" Maman objected. She had been born on one of the farms in the outlying district, and—even after twenty years—was still terrified of living in the village and overlooking the street. As far as I know, she had never been tempted to crack open the shutters and peek at the ghostly lady.

Papa balanced on his cane so he could pat Maman's hand. "It will be safe if we don't look down," he assured her.

It was Antoine who unfastened the shutters. Fifteen-year-old boys fear so little.

By then Grand-père had made his way around the table to the window. "Hélène," he greeted the widow. "What's the matter?"

"It's Jean-Pierre," she called, leaning out of her own kitchen window. "I dropped his medicine."

We all looked at each other. Jean-Pierre was her grandson. Although he was fully as big as Antoine, in reality he was only ten years old, and his thinking was that of a much younger child. For the past three years, the Widow Morin had been giving Jean-Pierre medicine that was supposed to make him smarter, though in three years none of us had seen a change. But that wasn't the medicine she was talking about.

"I was going to give him a dose of the medicine for his coughing," the Widow Morin explained, "and the bottle slipped out of my hand and broke."

We could hear Jean-Pierre coughing, sounding as though he'd break apart from the force of it. He'd been coughing since last winter, and with the new winter starting it had gotten worse. Jean-Pierre, who used to be so large, seemed to get thinner by the day.

The Widow Morin lowered her voice, as though we across the alley could hear without her grandson hearing. "I thought maybe we could make it through one night without, but..." She shook her head.

"What does she expect of us?" Maman demanded, louder than was necessary if she meant the question just for us.

"Hush," Papa whispered.

"What does she expect of us?" Maman repeated. I saw the Widow Morin's frantic look.

"I'll go get more medicine for Jean-Pierre," Grand-père assured her.

"No!" Maman said.

Grand-père gave Antoine's elbow a shove, and Antoine knew enough to smile politely, then close and bolt the shutters.

"Why should you risk yourself in the night?" Maman cried.

"Because Hélène is crippled by old age," Grand-père said. "And I am not."

"Pardon me," Maman said, "but you overestimate yourself."

"Hush!" Papa said again, this time not whispering. Grand-père was his father, not Maman's.

"Maman is right," Antoine said. Papa raised his hand to cuff him, but Antoine took a step back and said, "Grand-père, you are in remarkable condition for a man of seventy years, but I can make it from our doorstep to the corner in about half a minute. I think you have to admit that it would take you considerably longer." He turned to Papa. "And you, with your cane," he continued, "would take even longer than Grand-père." To Maman he said, "Surely you're not saying that none of us should go. Surely you're not saying that we should let Jean-Pierre die."

Maman looked as though that was exactly what she wanted to say.

I thought she was a horrid person. I thought Antoine was the bravest boy I'd ever heard of.

But Maman relented. "At least wait for her," Maman suggested. "Don't go out until after she walks by. That will improve your chances that you won't meet her."

"Your mother makes sense," Papa said, though some nights the ghostly lady came very late, and other nights she did not come at all. "Open the window to watch."

So Antoine opened the shutters over the street to watch for the lady. Then he opened the window over the alley to explain to the widow. "Madame Morin!" he called. "We will wait until the lady has passed..."

The widow cast a worried look back into her house, in the direction from which we could hear

Jean-Pierre coughing. Hesitantly, not daring to complain, she nodded her thanks.

If Gaetan and Mignon were hoping that the extraordinary circumstances would allow them to catch their first glimpses of the ghostly lady, Maman was too fast for them. She set me to helping them get ready for bed and said, "Afterward, Marianne, you and I will sit in the parlor. We'll keep each other awake."

The reason she suggested this was that there was a window in the north wall of the parlor that also looked out over the street. Maman didn't want the younger children sneaking out of their bedrooms for a peek while we were all in the kitchen, and she didn't trust me not to do the same by myself.

So once I saw the little ones firmly, if reluctantly, settled, we sat—Maman and I in the parlor; Antoine, Papa, and Grand-père in the kitchen. The only one who showed a tendency to sleepiness was Grand-père—a room away, I could hear him snoring. Periodically, Papa's injured foot must have bothered him, for I could hear him get up and move stiffly about the kitchen. It was during one of those times that I heard him say, suddenly, sharply, "Antoine! Antoine! Move away from the window!"

I jumped to my feet, and Maman was only a step behind me.

In the kitchen Antoine was at the front window, the one that faced the street, leaning against the sill, looking out with such intensity I knew what had to be out there.

Papa let his cane drop to the floor with a clatter as, dragging his foot behind, he tried to hurry across the distance that separated him from Antoine. Papa grabbed Antoine by the shoulder and hurled him away, then he slammed the street-side shutters closed.

"Jules?" we heard the widow call across. But she must have heard the commotion. She must have known what it was about, for she didn't open her own shutters.

"All is well," Grand-père shouted to her, looking from Papa to Antoine. From having fallen asleep with his head on the table, what hair he had was all sticking up.

"Fool," Papa called Antoine. "*Never* look at her eyes."

"I wasn't," Antoine protested, rubbing his shoulder where it had struck against the pantry door. But his gaze strayed back to the now-barred shutters.

"Fool," Papa repeated.

"What happened?" Maman demanded.

"She was halfway up the wall," Papa said.

"She'd just started up," Antoine objected.

Papa gave him a dark look, which Antoine could meet for just so long. Antoine turned away. "Where's my coat?" he asked.

I led him to it, right by the door where it always was. It was blue, with brass buttons, and it made him look quite respectable except for the shapeless felt cap he pulled from his pocket and put on his head.

"She was so beautiful," Antoine told me. "The last time I saw her, I was ten. I didn't remember her being so beautiful. I didn't realize how young she was."

I ignored his words. "I know what you need," I said, for the night air through the open window felt so cold. Almost a month too early, I brought out the woolen scarf I'd made to give Antoine for Christmas.

Antoine waited patiently while I placed the scarf just so around his neck.

"Be careful," I whispered to him.

"How many years have we been afraid of her?" he whispered back. "And what has she ever done?"

"Shh," I warned. If Maman heard talk like that, it would be the end of his errand for Jean-Pierre and his grandmother.

"Such a kind, sorrowful face," Antoine insisted. "Perhaps if just one person stopped to help her, maybe that would set her spirit to rest." Antoine's dark eyes were sad and concerned. Antoine always worried about other people, and of all the boys, he was the only one who had patience with Jean-Pierre.

But Papa had heard him, and Papa smacked him on the back of the head. In a whisper so that Maman wouldn't hear and worry, he said, "You're helping enough people tonight. If she comes, you forget this foolishness. You fly like the wind."

"Like the wind," Antoine assured us all, with his jaunty smile.

We opened the shutters and looked up and down the street. No sign of anyone between here and the corner to the right. No sign of anyone between here and where the street wound its way to the top of the hill to our left. That was the extent of the ghostly lady's realm: Whatever had bound her to this earth, she never went beyond the crest of the hill or around the corner, a total distance of four blocks, with many of the buildings built so close they touched.

With tears in her eyes, Maman kissed Antoine's cheeks. Drier eyed, Grand-père did the same. Papa shook Antoine's hand, and I heard him whisper, "No foolishness."

"Of course not," Antoine agreed.

I waved, and Gaetan, Mignon, and Honorée—up from their beds without any of us having noticed—chorused, "Good-bye, good luck," as Antoine raced confidently down the stairs.

"Still all clear," Grand-père shouted from the open kitchen window, and Antoine burst out of the front door.

He ran out into the middle of the street, but then instead of heading immediately to the corner, he turned to wave to us.

"Go," Papa said, gesturing him away. "Go!"

Antoine threw his cap in the air and called out a loud *"Whoop!"* so that when he would brag to his friends the next day about leaving the house during the hours of darkness, they'd know he spoke the truth.

Papa clapped his hand to his forehead in exasperation.

But Antoine took only that one extra moment.

Then, his blue coat flapping, his new scarf trailing behind, he ran to the corner—in under thirty seconds, by Grand-père's pocket watch, just as he had promised—and he disappeared from view.

Maman was so overwrought with Antoine's exuberance, she sat down in the parlor fanning herself, not even sending the younger ones back to bed. So we stayed in the kitchen with Papa and Grand-père. Anxiously, we stared out the window and waited.

Within a half hour there was a flurry of movement at the corner, and suddenly Antoine was back. With one hand he held on to his cap, because now he was running into the wind. He had his other hand in his coat pocket, by which we knew that he had succeeded in getting a new bottle of medicine from the doctor.

"Thank God," Papa said.

But a moment later he groaned.

I followed the direction of his gaze.

The ghostly lady was making her way down the hill toward us.

"Antoine!" Papa shouted.

Ten houses away, Antoine slowed down. Obviously he didn't hear. He took his hand down from his cap to press against his side. He must have run all the way back from the doctor's home, and now —when he most needed speed—he was winded.

Being higher up, we could see the ghostly lady was fast approaching, but Antoine could not.

"Antoine!" Grand-père and I and the children added our voices to Papa's.

Maman heard all our noise, and she came rushing into the kitchen. She added her voice to ours, and Antoine's head swiveled in our direction. He stopped entirely. He grinned—I could see the flash of his teeth in the moonlight—and he held up the bottle for us to see.

"Run!" we shouted.

He tipped his head quizzically and pointed to his ear, indicating he couldn't hear. He probably thought we were cheering.

We pointed frantically in the direction of the hill.

From where he stood, I don't think he could see her yet, but he finally realized what we were saying.

Continuing to our house was closer than going back to the safety of the corner. He jammed the bottle of Jean-Pierre's medicine into his pocket and took off at a run, so that his cap flew off his head and landed unheeded on the cobblestones behind him.

The lady was moving at an impossibly fast speed.

Other shutters were open, other people were shouting, "Run!"

The lady had reached the part of the street that leveled off, three houses to our left. Antoine was three houses to our right. But she was moving much faster than he.

Antoine was two houses away when she reached our building.

—when she stopped directly in front of our door.

—when she stood, her arms extended, blocking the way in.

Antoine stopped also, with no way to get around her.

Grand-père shouted, "Don't look at her eyes, boy!"

Then the ghostly lady took a step toward Antoine.

Antoine backed away.

But the lady's steps seemed to take her twice as

far as Antoine's, and the distance between them was quickly disappearing.

The door to the hat shop across the street from the butcher flew open. "Antoine, here!" called Mademoiselle Cosette, who owned the shop.

The ghostly lady practically flew at the door, and Mademoiselle Cosette slammed it shut just in time.

This gave Antoine the chance to race ahead several meters, but in another moment the lady had caught up with him.

"Your eyes!" several neighbors shouted down.

Antoine raised his arm to cover his eyes.

The ghostly lady stood in front of him, but every time she tried to pull his arms down, her hands would pass right through him.

I stayed at the window just long enough to make sure that Antoine seemed safe so long as he wasn't looking at her. Cosette had given me an idea. If I could open our door for Antoine, that would save him several seconds and might be enough to make a difference. I raced down the stairs and cracked open our front door.

Antoine was still standing on the street, frustratingly close, his arms covering his eyes.

The ghostly lady was still ineffectively trying to get his eyes uncovered. But she was obviously confused, or distracted, by all the open shutters, all the doors open a crack, all the people—besides Antoine—within easy reach.

Across the way and down a shop and a half, Cosette saw me peeking out our door. She'd always liked my brother though she was several years older. Now she called out, "Antoine! Can you walk with your eyes closed? Can you follow the sounds of our voices?"

Angrily, the ghostly lady rushed at her a second time.

At which point I screamed, "Antoine! Home!"

Cosette's door slammed yet again, and the lady spun around as Antoine leapt up the three steps separating our door from the street.

If there had been one step instead of three, he might have made it.

As it was, the lady stepped into the doorway, between the two of us.

I raised my hands to cover my eyes, but after a moment I peeked, for I had the impression that she was facing Antoine, not me.

I was right.

Antoine had his hands up, too. The lady had her hands resting, more or less, on his, though I could see she wasn't solid: Her dress, constantly billowing, passed through my legs and Antoine's; her long, unbound hair streamed about her, and I felt nothing where it passed through my arms.

There was no way she could harm us.

Then, so soft I tried to believe I hadn't really heard her, she spoke, for the first time in memory.

She said: "Please."

Antoine, who was kind even to simpleminded Jean-Pierre, slowly lowered his hands. I could see his face, not hers. But, through my fingers, I could tell he was looking directly into her eyes. He held out his hand to her, and this time her fingers clasped solidly about his. And then he became as transparent as she, and they both disappeared.

There's a street in the village where I grew up that everyone knows not to travel down past sunset.

But we don't live there anymore, for my mother finally got her wish, and my father moved the family to the town across the river.

For it was bad enough dealing with a sad, pale lady. But none of us could bear the thought of the ghost who had replaced her, with his sad brown eyes and the brass buttons of his coat twinkling in the moonlight as his woolen scarf billows in the breeze, which isn't necessarily there.

To Converse with the Dumb Beasts

KEDRIC WAS A GAME WARDEN who lived and worked on the king's hunting preserve. Though he enjoyed tending the animals, he did get lonely, for he had no family and his only companions were a dog and a cat, who had both lived with him for years.

One day, as Kedric was walking through the woods, he came upon a little old woman who was being chased by a bear. Knowing that, normally, bears don't chase people, Kedric looked more closely. A moment later he realized that somehow the woman had gotten between a mother bear and her cub; and the more the woman ran, the more the cub ran, with—of course—the bigger bear chasing after both.

Without stopping to worry about his own danger, Kedric leapt forward and pulled the woman out from between the two bears.

The mother bear grunted once as she passed them, then continued crashing through the trees after her cub.

Kedric guided the old woman to a stump so that she could sit down. "You just got that mama bear worried you were going to hurt her cub," he explained to calm her.

"I was worried that mama bear was going to hurt *me*," the woman gasped once she'd caught her breath. "I heard her keep saying, 'My baby, my baby,' but I couldn't see the little one, and I didn't know what she was talking about."

Kedric thought this was a strange thing to say and repeated, tugging at his earlobe as though that could help him hear better, "She kept saying...?"

" 'My baby, my baby,' " the old woman repeated. Then she added, "I do believe you saved my life."

"It was nothing," Kedric said. "She kept saying...?"

The old woman reached into the folds of her dress and pulled out an acorn. "I put a magic spell on this acorn," she explained. "Whoever owns it can understand the speech of beasts." She shook her head. "Not much help, was it?" She drew her arm back, and Kedric realized she was about to throw the acorn away.

"Wait!" he cried. A moment later, when the old woman looked at him, he felt foolish, for he didn't really believe that there was such a thing as a magic acorn that let people understand what animals said.

And yet, he thought, *and yet...*

Sometimes he grew so lonely, with only the cat and the dog to keep him company, and during the long evenings he would watch them—sitting there, watching him—and he would look into their deep, expressive eyes and wonder what they were thinking, what they would say if they could speak. He could risk being foolish for the chance to know.

The old woman was still studying him. Holding up the acorn, she asked, "You want this?" as if the thought were incredible.

"Please," Kedric said. "If you're through with it."

"Oh yes." The woman dropped the acorn into his hand. "But that's hardly a fitting reward for saving my life. May I offer you some other spell in addition?"

Kedric shook his head, feeling *very* foolish now that he actually held the acorn in his hand.

"Well, but I *am* grateful," the old woman said. "Good-bye and good luck," and with that she stood and nodded and began walking in the same direction she'd been running, following the river that flowed through the woods, down the hill, and eventually led—so Kedric had heard—to the sea.

Kedric was glad he'd taken the acorn, because the woman was obviously poor and had just as obviously wanted to reward him for saving her from the bear. Whether the acorn allowed him to understand the speech of animals, it had already accomplished something.

Kedric turned to continue on his way, and a bird swooped in front of him to land on a tree by the side of the river.

"My tree," the bird chirped. "My tree, my tree, my tree."

Kedric almost ran after the old woman. But she knew the acorn worked. *He* was the one who hadn't believed.

"Don't worry, little friend," Kedric assured the bird. "I won't try to take over your tree."

"My tree," the bird called back to him. "My tree."

Kedric closed his eyes to listen better and heard other birds calling out, "My tree," or, sometimes, "My branch," or, once in a great while, "Bug!"

So, Kedric thought, *birds don't have much to say.* But he was sure his pets would.

As he hurried home, there was talk all around him. But none of it was interesting. The butterflies constantly murmured to themselves, "Sip, sip, I'm sipping nectar, now I'm fluttering, flutter, flutter, now I'm sipping, sip, sip, now I'm fluttering." And the squirrels were too busy playing to pay attention to him. They chirped, "Wheee!" as they jumped from branch to branch. And, of course, the birds continued to call, "My branch." Kedric stopped only once, when a chipmunk darted across his path, chattering, "Winter's coming—gotta store."

"Winter's seven months away," Kedric called after the chipmunk.

But the chipmunk only paused for a moment. Its cheeks full of seeds so that its voice was garbled, it still clearly insisted, "Winter's coming," and dashed off.

As Kedric hurried up the path to his house, the dog must have heard him. "My house," the dog barked.

"Oh no," Kedric said, thinking of the single-minded birds.

But as soon as Kedric entered, the dog began jumping up and down and excitedly proclaimed, "My master, my master."

"Well, hello," Kedric said, delighted.

"My master's home early," the dog barked. "Is it because Master loves me? Sorry I drooled on Master—it's because I'm so excited. Does Master love me?"

As soon as Kedric reached down to pat the dog's head, the dog dropped to the floor and rolled over to expose his belly.

"Welcome, Master, am I cute? Do you love me?"

"Why, yes and yes, assuredly," Kedric said, scratching the dog's belly.

While he was doing that, the cat walked into the room. "Is he here to feed us?" she purred.

Kedric was surprised at the question. "Didn't I feed you this morning?" he asked, wondering if he had somehow forgotten.

"Pay attention to me," the dog said.

The cat told the dog. "Get out of his way. He's trying to get to the food to feed me."

And for the first time Kedric realized that while he could understand animals, animals couldn't understand him.

"I was sure I fed you this morning," he said anyway, by way of apology.

As he stepped over the dog and walked into the kitchen, the cat walked back and forth in front of his feet, saying, "He *is*. He *is* going to feed us. He's going to the feeding room."

The dog said, "Hey, look at me. Doesn't Master love me anymore?"

"Yes, yes," Kedric said. In the kitchen, he saw that there was still food in the cat's bowl. "You are *not* starving," he pointed out to her.

She rubbed against his leg and meowed, "Are you going to feed me? Are you going to feed me now?"

Kedric gave her some fresh food, in case there

was something wrong with what he'd given her in the morning, but she only nibbled. "Nothing new, nothing exciting," she complained. "You said he was home early. I thought that meant something new and exciting to eat."

"Is the master going to play with me now?" the dog said. "Ooo, I've got an itch"—he began biting at his side—"but I'll be ready to play in a moment."

Kedric pointed at the cat. "You are spoiled," he said.

"He's pointing at me," the cat said. "Do you think he's got food behind that finger?"

"Stop talking about food!" Kedric shouted. "You've got food!"

They might not have understood the words, but they knew shouting. "Good," the dog said. "Now Master's mad at you; he'll love me more. He'll think *you* chewed up that shoe."

"He's shouting because he's trying to tell me where there's food," the cat said.

"Stop it!" Kedric said. "Stop all this mindless chattering." Disappointed, he sat down at the kitchen table and rested his face in his hands. He was aware of the dog and the cat each looking at him with their large soulful eyes.

The dog said, "Is Master sick? Is Master unhappy? If I chase my tail, will that make Master feel better?" The dog began to chase its tail.

The cat said, "Do you really think he's sick? If he dies, do you think we should eat him?"

Kedric jumped up from his chair. He threw the acorn down on the floor and stomped on it until it broke into little pieces.

This didn't help. He distinctly heard the dog say, "I can do that, too!" Then the dog ran through the pile of crumbled pieces, scattering them all across the floor.

"*I* don't think he's dying," the cat said. "We'll never get to eat him."

Kedric clapped his hands to his ears. "Aaaaagh!" he cried. Maybe it wasn't too late to catch up to the old woman, to ask her to come back and take the spell off the acorn, since breaking it obviously wasn't enough, and now he could never find all the pieces.

"Fine game!" the dog cried. "Master's so clever! I can play, too! Aaa-rooooo!" But the dog couldn't run and cover his ears at the same time, and he kept tipping over.

"This is squirrel food," the cat complained, sniffing at the remains of the acorn. "This isn't for us to eat."

Still holding his hands over his ears, Kedric ran screaming out of his house and down the path. The door didn't slam behind him until he was halfway across the clearing and into the woods.

The dog and the cat looked at each other in the silence of the house.

"Was it something I said?" the dog asked, biting at his itch again. "Doesn't Master love me any-more?"

"Don't worry," the cat assured him. She began to lick herself clean. "He just went to find better food."

BOY WITCH

CLARENCE'S MOTHER was a famous witch. The three of them—Clarence and his parents—lived in a cottage that was near several villages but not in any one of them. People came to buy spells and healing potions, to have their fortunes told, and to ask advice. Clarence's mother specialized in good magic, so if she used a spell to remove stones from one farmer's fields, she made sure they didn't show up in his neighbor's, and she only worked weather spells if everybody in the region agreed on what they needed.

"There are enough sorrows in the world without me making more," she would tell anybody who asked for something that would harm another. "Magic is complicated enough already without setting out to do ill."

One day in earliest spring, the snow was melting

so fast that several villages sent to Clarence's mother to say they were in danger of being flooded. As Clarence's father hitched up the wagon to take her from one overflowing creek to another, he told Clarence, "We'll be gone all day and maybe into tomorrow. You're more than old enough to be on your own and to take care of the animals"—for they kept several, since Clarence's mother didn't make enough money as a witch to support the family.

"I can do that," Clarence assured them.

"Be good," Clarence's mother said, which she always did, and Clarence said he would. Then he stood in the doorway and waved good-bye as his parents rode off in the wagon. He milked the goats, then let them loose in the meadow. So far, so good. He fed the chickens and the pigs, and everything went fine there, and he was just sitting down to his own breakfast when someone knocked on the door and called, "Hello. Anybody home?"

Clarence got up and found that his visitor was a girl who looked about sixteen or seventeen years old, which was three or four years older than he was. She was *very* pretty. "Hello," he said to her. "Who are you?"

The girl tugged nervously at the scarf that covered her head, as though to make sure that it covered every bit of her hair—which it did. "My name is Emma," she said. "I'm looking for the woman who's a witch."

"She's not here," Clarence said. "She won't be back until tomorrow."

"Oh." The girl's voice was little more than a sigh. "Never mind, then." But her shoulders drooped as she turned to walk away, and Clarence could tell that tomorrow would be too late.

He called after her, "Is there anything I can do to help?"

The girl Emma whirled around and asked, "Are you a witch, too?"

There was such hope and awe and delight in her tone, Clarence felt very important. He stood straight, which made him almost as tall as Emma, and he said, "Yes," which wasn't exactly true. His mother said he had talent, but she also said magic was too important and too dangerous to play with. "When you are entirely grown up," Clarence's mother would tell him, "when you can understand the consequences and know how to weigh the choices, *then* I will teach you."

But now, seeing the way Emma looked at him with such respect, he said, "Yes, I am a witch, too."

But then Emma began to look suspicious. "You seem very young," she said in the same tone his mother used when she thought he'd done something especially foolish.

"Actually," Clarence said, "I'm one hundred and seven years old. This is the appearance I give myself magically."

That impressed her, he could tell, more than a thirteen-year-old boy who wasn't even apprenticed yet.

Emma tugged once more on her scarf to make sure it was secure, then she said, "I want to buy a magic spell from you. Can you do magic?"

"Of course," Clarence said, eager to please. "But I need to know what you want done. Our family doesn't believe in doing harmful magic." He said this to prepare her for her disappointment later, when he would say that the spell she asked for would have far-reaching consequences.

The girl began to cry. "I don't want harmful magic," she told Clarence. "I just want my hair back."

"Your hair?" he repeated, taking a closer look at the scarf.

Emma pulled the scarf down, and Clarence saw that her hair had been cut off in ragged chunks so that it was shorter than a boy would wear it. "My brother did this, for a joke, while I was asleep," she told him. She used her scarf to blow her nose. "You see, today I'm supposed to meet the young man I'm to marry, the son of an old friend of my father's. He's coming to our village this afternoon. We've never met before, and I'm afraid"—she began crying all over again—"I'm afraid if he sees me looking like this, he'll call it all off."

"Oh," Clarence said, "I'm sure he wouldn't..." But he drifted off, not sounding convincing, because he wasn't sure at all: She *did* look frightful, especially with her nose all red and runny.

"It wouldn't take much of a spell to make my hair grow back, would it?" Emma said.

"I—" Clarence caught himself before he said, "I wouldn't think so," and he said, instead, "I'm sure we'll find just the right spell for you." His mother had all sorts of books and scrolls, and he hoped one of them would say something about growing hair, for surely making hair grow could have no consequences, and he very much wanted to impress this girl who—with longer hair and a dry nose—would be beautiful.

But even the answer Clarence gave made Emma suspicious. "*Find* the right spell?" she asked. "Haven't you done this before?"

"Certainly," Clarence said. "Lots of times. But...uh, it all depends on the conjunction of the planets, and atmospheric conditions on the particular day of the spell, and...well, too many things that someone as young as you would never understand."

Emma looked impressed again.

"Come inside," Clarence said. "Have some tea while you wait."

Emma came in and sat down on a stool at the kitchen table, but she grew impatient as Clarence piled book after book on the table and looked through scroll after scroll. "You don't seem very well organized," she told him. "You don't seem to know where to begin to look."

"As a matter of fact," Clarence said, hoping not to sound too relieved, "I have it right here." In one of the ancient books, he had found a heading that said:

> For Thick, Longe hair for a Younge
> Personne Without Anye Yet

And there was a subheading that promised hair "fully down to ye waist," with adjustments to the spell for those who preferred longer or shorter.

Clarence looked again at Emma's head. Well, she was young, and she had hardly any hair left. This was probably a spell to make a baby's hair grow in faster, he thought, but it certainly seemed to fit Emma perfectly anyway. "Waist length?" he asked.

"Oh yes," Emma agreed.

"Now, let's see...," Clarence said. He read the incantation out loud, sounding the words out, making the proper gestures that were drawn in the margins of the book.

Emma screamed and fell backward off her stool.

Clarence ran around the table to help her up and saw that the hair on her head had not changed at all. But Emma had grown a beard—a Thick, Longe beard—that reached to her waist.

"Oops," he said.

"What have you done?" she screamed, feeling the lower part of her face, as though she couldn't quite believe that the long beard she could see was actually attached to her.

"I think we need to make a slight adjustment here," Clarence admitted. He hoped that the next page in the book would say:

For Getting Rid of Thick, Longe hair

But it didn't. It was something about how to get gravy stains out of wool.

He looked through the next several pages. Emma continued to scream all the while, which was quite distracting. "Well, if you're going to be that way about it," he said, "we'll just cut it off and start all over again." He got out his mother's sewing scissors, but every time he cut off a section of Emma's beard, it grew right back again.

"It's a magic beard, you idiot," she told him, snatching the scissors out of his hand. "You'll have to take it away magically."

"You may be right," Clarence said. "Just calm down. Are you calm now?" He didn't like the way she was looking at him while she still held the scissors. "*I* have the magic power," he said, to remind her that she needed him, "the books have the words. I'll find the right words." She finally let him take the scissors back.

"Let's see..." Clarence frantically looked through his mother's papers. "Ah! Here we go!" He'd found an entry in another book that said:

hair Removal

The book told him what words to say and instructed him to wiggle his fingers at the part of the body from which he wanted to remove the hair. ("Syche as," the book said, "ye limbs, ye back, ye face, &c.")

Clarence said the words and wiggled his fingers at Emma's face.

The beard promptly disappeared. So did her eyebrows and eyelashes and most of the hair that had been left on her head.

"Oops," Clarence said, trying to make the gesture smaller. Too late.

"What *oops*?" Emma said. She felt the bottom of her face, but then her hands drifted up around her eyes and forehead, and she began screaming again.

"Wait, wait, it's all right," Clarence said. "Look." He held up a scroll, pointing, then read it out loud in case Emma couldn't read.

Moving Thyngs

"I'd like to move you right out of here," Emma told him.

"No," Clarence said. "Don't you see? We'll do the spell to make the beard again, then move tiny bits of the beard to your eyebrows, and the rest to your head."

Emma thought about this. "No . . . ," she started, but by then Clarence had relocated the For Thick, Longe Hair for a Younge Personne Without Anye Yet spell.

"Trust me," he told her, and once again he said the incantation.

Once again the beard appeared on her chin, looking even more foolish then before in the absence of eyebrows and lashes. Then Clarence read the incantation for moving things—moving, as he read, a wisp of beard above either eye, and the rest of the beard to the top of her head.

"How does it look?" Emma asked.

"Fine," Clarence told her, though in truth it looked as though she had tiny beards for eyebrows, and the beard on top of her head stuck straight up in the air and ended in a point, just like an upside-down beard.

Wisely, Emma didn't take Clarence at his word. She touched her head, and a low growl started deep in her throat. "Where's a mirror?" she asked. "I demand to see a mirror." Her fingers found her eyebrows, and she began to twitch.

"We're not quite ready for a mirror yet," Clarence admitted. He began looking frantically through the books while Emma muttered, "Where are those scissors?" and rummaged through his mother's sewing supplies.

"Here we go!" Clarence announced. He'd found a spell called:

Rich Golden hair

The bits and pieces on Emma's head were blond. This was sure to work. She'd probably look better than she had before.

Clarence recited the incantation. Emma tipped over and fell to the floor again with a loud *clunk!*

"What happened?" Emma asked somewhat groggily from the floor.

"Nothing," Clarence said.

But Emma reached up and touched her head. "Why is my hair metal?" she demanded.

"Actually," he admitted, "it's turned to gold." It still looked like an upside-down beard, except that now it was a solid chunk of gold. "It'll be worth a fortune," he pointed out. "You can knock pieces out of it, and new pieces will grow back—just like it did when we tried cutting it off with the scissors. You and your new husband will be rich. Neither one of you will ever have to work again."

Emma grabbed Clarence by the front of his shirt. Very softly she said, "Get. It. Off. Now."

"Yes," Clarence assured her. "I'm pretty sure

I already came across that spell, if you'll just loosen your hold so I can look—actually, so I can breathe..."

Emma let go.

Clarence found a spell called:

Sticky Fingers

which said it was good for picking up anything, and the spell on the next page said:

Loose Fingers

which he checked, beforehand, to make sure it was good for letting go of anything, rather than for having fingers actually become loose. But, just to be on the safe side, Clarence said the magic words while pointing to Emma rather than to himself to give *her* the Sticky Fingers.

"Now," he said, "take hold of the hair on top of your head."

"Beard," she corrected him. "It's a beard." She took hold of it, and it came off in her hands, and no more came back since it had been removed magically.

Clarence breathed a sigh of relief.

"It's stuck," Emma said, realizing she couldn't let go of the large golden cone.

"It's taken care of," Clarence told her. And he recited the Loose Fingers spell, so that the beard dropped from her hands. At this point she still had tiny little beard eyebrows, no eyelashes, and less hair on her head than she had started with.

"Let's see," Clarence said, leafing through the books and picking up various scrolls. "Here's one."

"What does it say?" Emma demanded.

Clarence picked up the scroll, one of the oldest, and read:

"A Spelle for Hayre"

The instructions said that, if such was important, the conjurer could specify location for the Hayre, colour, or size.

"Size?" Emma asked suspiciously. *"Size?"*

Clarence shrugged. "Size, quantity, length—means the same thing. You'll be wanting *big*."

Emma started to shake her head, but already Clarence was saying the words.

The next thing he knew, Emma had a big blond-colored rabbit attached to her head.

Emma fainted.

The rabbit didn't seem too happy, either.

Why, oh why did I ever start this? Clarence asked himself.

He sat down at the table and began reading the books more carefully rather than trying to skim through. Eventually he found what he needed. The spell was called:

Reversing Your Previous Enchantment

Clarence said the spell, and the rabbit disappeared. He said the spell again, fervently hoping that it wouldn't simply undo the reversal. It didn't. The gold beard, which was lying on the floor next to the fainted Emma, rolled into her hands, because he'd just reversed the Loose Fingers spell, which left her, once again, with Sticky Fingers. Clarence said the words again and again to reverse himself through each spell until finally Emma's beard disappeared, but her eyebrows and eyelashes stayed so that she looked just as she had when she'd first come in.

Which was where he had started.

"Emma," he said, shaking her shoulder. "Emma."

Her eyes fluttered opened. Seeing him, she shrieked.

"I hope this has been a lesson to you," he said, which was actually something his mother liked to say to him. As though this was all part of some grand plan he had had, he said, "You should be satisfied with what you have. If your young man does not appreciate you for what you are, he isn't worth having."

"If my young man is nothing like you," Emma answered, "I *will* be satisfied." Without even tying her scarf back around her head, she stomped out of the house.

Clarence spent the rest of the morning putting order back in his mother's papers, picking up the articles from her sewing basket that Emma had scattered, cleaning up the food that had spilled on and around the table. He milked the goats again, said hello to the pigs, gathered the chickens' eggs, prepared a lunch for himself, and sat down to eat.

And waited, hoping somebody else would come.

LOST SOUL

SHE WAS SITTING ON THE ROCK, smiling to herself, her feet dangling in the stream, and he thought she was the loveliest sight he had ever seen. She leaned backward, bracing her feet on the rock, and arched her back so that a hand span or two of her long hair dipped into the water, where the current gently tugged at it. She closed her eyes against the brightness of the sun, but still she smiled. It was wonderful to see her, he thought, to see someone so obviously in love with life.

She straightened, laughing, and shook her head so that crystal beads of moisture flew in the afternoon light. Her hair was the color of the wheat ripening in the field he had inherited when his father had died.

The wheat... a little voice reminded him. It was time for harvesting the wheat. There was work to be done, which he had put off to visit his ailing grandmother, half a morning's walk away from home. He had stayed as long as he could but left because a harvest cannot wait. Though he was eighteen years old and though he had spent his entire life helping his father, or planting and harvesting on his own, at the moment he found it difficult to remember what it was he had to do.

This forest was said to be haunted by spirits eager to devour an unwary man's soul. But he was a Christian and he knew a man's soul was his own, so he stepped out from the trees and into the clearing.

Still smiling, she gazed directly into his eyes.

He had thought she might be startled. "Excuse me," he might have said then. "I didn't mean no harm," he could have said, and come forward to show that he was, in fact, harmless. Something— something—to get started. But she only sat there, her eyes as cool and green as the stream, the smile still on those pretty lips.

"Ahm," he said, and could go no further without shuffling his feet and twisting the cap he clutched in his sweaty hands—just like the time ten or eleven summers back when he'd been caught pitching pebbles at the swans in the baron's moat.

She tipped her head and looked at him quizzically. "Yes?" she asked, still smiling.

A lady. He could tell by the way she said just

that one word. A lady, despite the unbound hair and the bare feet and the plain green dress trailing in the stream. And here he was coming up to her in the woods, bold as anything, and her people no doubt just a shout away, ready to come tearing out of wherever they were waiting for her and beat him for presumption.

"Uh," he said.

"Oh," she said. "I see. *Ahm. Uh.* That must be how you charm the girls—by telling them such sweet, pretty things."

He felt his face go red, despite the fact that she had still never stopped smiling. "No," he mumbled.

"No?" she repeated. "*No,* you don't charm girls, or *no,* you don't tell them sweet, pretty things?"

He had no idea how to answer in a way that wouldn't make him out to be a fool. "Ahm..."

"Oh, back to *ahm.*" She leaned back, supporting her weight on her arms, stretching slowly and deliberately.

He forced his gaze back to her face and saw that she was well aware of where he had been looking. And was pleased by it, he realized with a jolt of surprise, just as she patted the rock and said, "Come and sit by me, boy, and tell me some more sweet, pretty things."

Boy. Even though he was a man by any standard, with his own holding, which he had farmed successfully for almost two years now. Even though they looked to be much of an age. For the briefest instant he was angry, but she was still smiling at him, and he was finding it hard to breathe.

Because of the way she was sitting, he would have to step into the stream to get around her to the other side of the rock. Should he take off his boots? It only made sense, but then she would see that his feet were dirty and callused. She whose feet were white and smooth and beautifully shaped. He tore his gaze from her feet and stepped—boots and all—into the water, which was colder than he had anticipated. There was an undercurrent, too, so he teetered out of balance and sat more quickly than he had intended.

"You're sitting on my hair, boy," she said.

"I'm sorry," he breathed, and stood long enough to brush away a long, golden strand. It was soft and smooth and fine and it smelled wonderful—*she* smelled wonderful: like the first day of spring after a hard winter.

She leaned forward to wring the edge of her dress, and her arm brushed against his. He didn't dare move. She looked back at him over her shoulder, then fanned the skirt of the dress, exposing long, shapely legs. Her skin was pale.

Like ivory, he thought. Not that he had ever seen ivory, but "skin like ivory" was what the ballad singers always said. So much more beautiful than the tanned legs of the girls in the village or those who worked their fathers' holdings.

She left the hem up near her knees. "You're shivering, boy," she pointed out. "The water's not that cold."

It wasn't. But he said nothing.

"What's your name?" she asked.

"Quinton." He cleared his throat and repeated it.

She laughed. " 'Fifth-born,' " she said, which he already knew from the baron's chaplain. "Are you?"

It took a moment for the question to sink in. He nodded.

"How delightful." She laughed, and he ached from the beauty of the sound, though he had no idea why she laughed. He had never met anyone who talked like this, who acted like this.

"What's your name?" he asked.

Her green eyes sparkled as she looked him over. She waited just long enough for him to regret his brashness before she answered, "You may call me Salina."

"Salina," he murmured, trying out the sound of it.

"Do you like it?" she asked. "I just made it up." She put her hands around the back of her neck and lifted the mass of her hair so that it brushed against his arm. "It was very wicked of you to sit on my hair, Quinton," she said.

"It was an accident." *Don't be angry*, he begged mentally. "I didn't mean it."

"Of course you did, you wicked boy. You wanted to touch my hair."

"I didn't," he protested. "I swear."

"You didn't?" She looked at him soberly. "Don't you like my hair?"

"I..." Was she angry or not? "Yes," he whispered. *Oh, definitely yes.*

"Then you may touch it again." She turned her back to him, so that he was bedazzled by the sunlit goldenness of the hair. A waterfall of silken threads. She wasn't angry after all.

His hand shook, touching her shoulder.

"Now, Quinton." She looked back at him. "I said my hair."

He didn't know whether to say *Yes, Salina*, or *Yes, my lady*. So he only said, "Yes," and combed his fingers through her hair and was grateful that she couldn't see his rough, sun-browned hands.

She made soft, throaty sounds of approval and after a long while, leaned back against him, her hand resting lightly on his leg. He couldn't believe his good fortune, that this was happening to him. Her breathing was slow and regular, while his came faster and he had to concentrate to remember to keep his mouth closed. She was a lady, he reminded himself; he could lose everything by trying to go too fast. He worked his fingers upward, then let his hands linger on the back of her head, massaging. And when she seemed to like that, he strayed forward, to rub her temples. She settled more firmly against him, rubbing her shoulders against his chest, so he moved his hands down once more to her shoulders.

She whirled around and slapped him. "That's enough now," she said.

He sat back, surprised and dismayed. Had he been too rough? Or had she suddenly discerned what was on his mind? *She had to have known,* he thought. She had to have known what effect she was having on him.

She was shaking her hair out and rearranging her dress. He couldn't tell what she was thinking.

"Please," he whispered.

She didn't seem to hear him.

He looked away and saw that the sun was low in the sky. Almost dusk—where had the time gone?—and he was only halfway home. When he had first sat down, he had brought his feet up onto the side of the rock, but somehow, without his having noticed, they had ended up back in the water. They felt numb with the chill.

"Well?" Salina said.

He looked up.

"Will you be my gallant champion and carry me back to dry land?" She held her arms open, and very, very gently he picked her up. The current tugged even more strongly than he remembered, but she held tightly to his neck, which almost sent him into a panic of ecstasy.

Once back on the grassy shore, she asked, "Are you going to set me down, or will you hold me all night long?"

"Do I have a choice?" he asked.

"Silly boy. You *can* talk sweetly. Put me down."

He did, ache though he did to do so.

"Will you be back tomorrow?" she asked.

His heart thudded so hard he was sure it was about to burst. "Yes," he said. "Oh yes. Will you?"

"Perhaps," she said, "Quinton. You'll just have to come back and see." She turned quickly and walked into the woods.

"Wait." He took several steps, but already she was gone.

She didn't appear to have taken the path toward Woodrow, where his grandmother lived, nor the path toward his own Dunderry.

"Salina," he called into the darkening woods. She could be anywhere and he wouldn't see her in this light. "Lady Salina."

But all he saw was the dark bulk of the trees, and all he heard was the whisper of leaves.

It was dark by the time he reached his cottage on the forest side of Dunderry, but somebody had gotten a fire going: He could see the light around the edges of the door. *Who?* he wondered. Both his parents were dead, and the two sisters who had survived childhood had husbands and children of their own and wouldn't be here.

Salina, he thought, beyond all reason.

He flung the door open, and a dark-haired peasant jumped up from the pot she was tending over the fire. "Quinton!" she cried. "Are you all right?" She threw her arms around his neck, and for the longest time he couldn't think who this young woman might be.

"Ada," he said finally, pulling the name from a far corner of his memory. She smelled of stale earth and was suffocating him. He pulled away.

"Quinton?" Her voice grated despite the concern in its tone. "Did your grandmother...You were gone so long. She didn't...What happened?"

Did she know how ignorant she sounded? Did she know how stupid she looked with that worried expression? But that wasn't fair; she was only trying to be helpful. It wasn't her fault she was so dark and ugly and common.

"My grandmother?" he repeated.

"Quinton? Your poor sick grandmother, she didn't...die, did she?"

"No." Quinton looked into the pot of stew Ada had made for him. Beans and onions. Salina wouldn't have made him a supper of beans and onions.

"Quinton," Ada demanded.

"What?" He looked up at her. "My grandmother is fine."

"Then where were you? We were expecting you back by midafternoon. Where are the baron's draft horses?"

The horses. Now Quinton remembered. He was supposed to have brought the horses for the harvest tomorrow. He, Ada's father, and several others with holdings in the baron's northern lands were going to work together. "I forgot."

She gave him that dull, uncomprehending look again.

"I'll get them tomorrow."

Would she ever close her mouth?

"I forgot!" he screamed at her. "I'll get them to-morrow. I can't very well go now." Did he have to pick her up and throw her out the door to get her to leave? He remembered the feel of Salina in his arms and moaned.

"Quinton?" Ada sounded scared.

He got into the bed in the corner without even taking off his boots. He pulled the cover up to his chin although the night was warm enough to go without, and turned his back to her. "I'm all right," he said, to get her to leave. "I'll get the damn horses tomorrow."

He heard her hesitate, then take the pot off

the fire, then leave. He clutched the blanket and thought of Salina.

At first daylight he set out without breakfast. He saw Ada's father cutting through the wheat field but didn't pause. "I'm getting the horses," he shouted, waving, not stopping.

"Quinton!" he heard Hakon call, but he kept on walking. The baron's castle was to the east, but so was the stream where he had seen Salina. He'd go there first, then on to the castle afterward.

He didn't know how he had made it through the night without her. He hadn't slept at all. He had to see her again. Had to smell her. To touch her. *Please be there,* he thought. *Please be there.*

She wasn't.

It was still early. Perhaps he should have gotten the horses first. Maybe she would come only in the afternoon. He watched the sunlight sparkle on the stream and didn't dare leave for fear he'd miss her.

He lay down in the grass, torn between enjoying and being afraid of the sweet ache of thinking of Salina. *She'll come back,* he thought, *and I'll see that she's not all that I remember. Pretty, but there are a lot of pretty girls.*

He'd get over it. He'd get her out of his mind. Nobody, nobody could look that beautiful. Skin could not be that soft, that pale and radiant.

Eyes could not be that green and deep. Hair, lips, throat could not be that perfect, that inviting. To touch her just once, just once...

He woke with a start.

His face was pressed against the grass, but he could see that the moon was out, pale and low, sharing the late-afternoon sky with the sun. He lifted his head, turned to face the stream.

Salina was there, though he had never heard her come. She was sitting on the rock, in the same green dress, watching him with that day-brightening smile.

"Sleepy Quinton," she called. She stretched, standing on tiptoe, so that her tight-fitting dress seemed to cling to every curve of her body. Then she stepped onto the grass, standing close enough that he could have touched her. "I could easily grow to love you," she whispered. "In fact, I may love you already."

Before he could catch his breath, she disappeared into the trees.

"Salina!" He jumped to his feet. But she was already gone.

He had waited so long, to see her for such a short time. It wasn't fair. It wasn't fair.

He waded out into the stream, to the rock upon which she'd been sitting. It was still warm. He thought he could still smell the fresh scent of her there. He sank to his knees so that the cold water came up to his chest, and he put his cheek against her warmth on the rock.

By the time he got back to the cottage, night had once again fallen. Ada was waiting there for him, again, but this time so was her father.

"Quinton," Hakon said, putting a big hand on his shoulder and shaking him with a little less friendliness than his tone indicated. "Quinton, lad. What ails you?"

"Nothing," Quinton said. His clothes had not dried in the night air and he was shivering.

"You're fevered, lad."

Quinton pushed the older man's hand away.

"Where've you been?"

Quinton shrugged and turned his face from Ada and her father.

Hakon wouldn't be stopped. "I went to the castle," he said.

The horses. Quinton had forgotten yet again.

"I saw nary a sign of you along the way, and the second stable master said they'd not seen you either."

"No," Quinton said. He started to get undressed, hoping that would get them to leave. He kicked his boots off, then pulled his shirt up over his head.

Ada turned her back.

"I brung the horses," Hakon said.

Quinton took his pants off and crawled into bed, and still Hakon stood there staring at him.

"We done Rankin's holding in what was left of the day. We're doing Durward's tomorrow morning. And Osborn's and Halsey's, if we have the time. If you want yours done the day after, you'll be at Durward's with the rest of us."

Quinton didn't answer, and eventually the two of them left.

She wasn't there the next day, though Quinton got to the stream early and didn't leave at all. He spent the night out in the open, sleeping on the grass where she had stepped on her way from the rock to the forest. The next day dawned misty and rainy, and by late afternoon he was too cold and hungry to wait any longer.

At home he found a pot simmering over the fire. Ada. Wouldn't that girl leave him alone? As a matter of principle, he wanted not to eat what she had prepared; but principles don't ward off a chill. He ate the soup and the bread and crawled into bed.

"Salina." He said the name out loud, as though that would have more effect than just thinking it. "I hate you," he whispered into the night. "Come back. Come back." Tears ran down his face, and he was too tired to wipe them away.

The next morning Hakon was there before

Quinton had a chance to leave. "Quinton," he said. "We're willing to give you another chance."

Chance? Quinton thought, fastening his boot. *Chance?*

"You having some kind of woman trouble?"

Quinton snorted, shifted to his other boot.

"Ada— Ada, she been outside your door last night. She said to her mother she heard you calling some woman's name."

"It's none of your business, old man."

Hakon grabbed his arm. "See here," he said, all pretense of concern, of friendliness, gone. "You done made promises to my girl. Certain things are expected of you."

"Leave me alone."

Hakon held on to him.

I could easily grow to love you, Salina had said. *In fact, I may love you already.* She was no doubt waiting for him even now. And this old fool was keeping him from her.

"Let go of me," he cried.

"You're not going nowhere," Hakon said. "You're going to stay here and work your father's holding and do right by my girl."

Quinton snatched up the heavy pot in which Ada had cooked the soup. "I don't want your ugly little daughter," he said, shoving the pot at Hakon. "Take this and get out of here."

"You damn well better want her," Hakon said.

"I'll go to the baron. I'll tell him what you promised, and he'll see to it you marry her proper or lose your rights to this land."

Quinton didn't care about the land. He didn't care about anything except getting out of there, of getting to Salina. But Hakon wouldn't let go. Quinton swung the pot and hit him across the side of the head.

The old man dropped.

Quinton straightened his shirt, which had gotten pulled down over his shoulder. *Salina,* he thought. Salina was waiting.

Shortly before he reached the edge of the forest, he heard footsteps running up behind him. "Quinton," a female voice called. He turned and faced her: a dark girl, unlike his Salina of the sunlight. She had dark eyes, dark hair, even her skin was darkened by years of toiling under the sun. Soon, another few years, it would be wrinkled and cracked and sagging—youth did not last long in the northern holdings. He couldn't put a name to the girl who clutched at him and begged him to return.

"Who is she?" this ugly walnut of a girl demanded. "Nobody lives in the forest, Quinton. Not real people. You've found some wood sprite or a naiad, one of the old folk."

He kept on walking, though she pulled his sleeve loose at the shoulder.

"Quinton, she'll steal your soul away."

That was ridiculous. A soul was a soul. How could it be stolen away, like a loaf of bread or a pair of boots? He didn't bother to tell this girl that. He told her: "Look to your father."

"Quinton?" She stood there with that vacant expression on her homely face, looking from him to his cottage, back to him.

Once he saw that she wasn't following him into the woods, he didn't look back.

He found Salina where he'd first seen her: on the rock by the stream. But this time she wasn't alone.

There was a young boy with her, sitting on her rock in what should have been Quinton's place. A peasant, he saw. An ugly, dirty little peasant. He was an overgrown child of perhaps thirteen or fourteen, and he was finger-combing Salina's beautiful golden hair.

"Salina!" Quinton cried.

She turned, languorously, to look over her shoulder at him and smile. "Quinton," she said, her voice as empty as her eyes and her smile. "My pretty-speeched young sleeper. Have you dreamt of me lately?"

Quinton strode into the water, fighting the pull of the current. The peasant boy didn't even have the decency to appear frightened of him. His eyes were dull and unresponsive, and he continued to comb his fingers through Salina's hair as though unaware of anything else. Quinton's gaze went from Salina's lovely face, past her shoulder, down the length of her arm, to her hand resting on the boy's thigh. Apparently she wasn't concerned that he was ugly or little more than a child.

Quinton grabbed him by the collar and hauled him off the rock, staggering against the pull of the current. He flung the young peasant into the water in the general direction of the shore. At least the boy had wit enough to scramble to his feet.

"Tomorrow," Salina called to him. "Come back tomorrow."

The boy ran off into the forest.

Quinton looked from his retreating back to Salina and saw his life collapse in front of him. "You said you loved me," he said.

"I lied," she told him.

"But I love you."

"I know."

"Please—"

"Don't beg," she snapped. "Begging is for cripples and dogs."

"Salina..." He trailed off at the look on her face.

"Boy?" she said, laughing.

"I gave up everything for you."

"And I have nothing to give you in return." She held her arms open. "Did I ask you for everything?"

"Don't laugh at me," he said, and she laughed

at him again. "Don't you laugh!" he screamed. And still she laughed.

He grabbed her by the hair and dragged her into the water. She didn't even struggle, she was laughing so hard. He pushed her backward and held her down so that her face was under the water, and even that didn't get the smile off her face. Her hair streamed out, looking green and feathery. And the smile never left her face, even long after she had to have been dead.

He staggered to the shore, repulsed by what he had done, repulsed because of the sense of exhilaration he felt, repulsed because he didn't know if that had come from being pressed against her or from killing her.

I'll go back to Dunderry, he thought. He remembered Ada's sweet face and thought with horror of the way he had treated her. He'd tell her . . . He remembered her father and sank to his knees. Had he struck the old man hard enough to kill him? There was no way of telling. Not without going back to see.

"Hey!" a voice called.

He jerked up his head to see two men on horseback. The baron's guards, judging by their chain mail.

"You Quinton Redmonson?" one of them asked.

"No." He shook his head and backed away.

Hakon must be dead. Ada must have gone to the castle and told them what had happened. "No," he repeated. He felt the incline of the ground where it dipped down to the stream.

The man pointed a finger at him. "You. Get back here."

Could they see Salina's body? he wondered. He couldn't. Had the current carried her away already? He could argue that killing Hakon had been an accident. But would they believe two accidents in one day? The cold water lapped at his ankles, his knees.

"I said—"

But he missed the last of what the baron's man said, because his foot slipped in the muck at the bottom of the stream and he fell. For an instant he came up sputtering, then the water closed over his head again.

It isn't this deep, he thought. *It isn't this deep.* He was facing upward. He could see the sunlight hitting the surface of the stream, but he couldn't get to it.

The water roared in his ears, pressed down against his face. *Salina,* he thought. Salina was holding him down. But that was foolishness. There was nothing there. All he had to do was sit up. It was only the water pressing down on him. Water no deeper than Salina's hair was long. Water that pressed down on him until he didn't want to sit up after all.

He stopped struggling. He let the water in. Up above, the sunlight danced a golden green dance. The last thing he saw was her; the last thing he thought of was her.

She was sitting on the rock, smiling to herself, her feet dangling in the stream, and he thought she was the loveliest sight he had ever seen. She leaned backward, bracing her feet on the rock, and arched her back so that a hand span or two of her long hair dipped into the water, where the current gently tugged at it. She closed her eyes against the brightness of the sun, but still she smiled. It was wonderful to see her, he thought, to see someone so obviously in love with life.

REMEMBER ME

I FIND MYSELF KNEELING on the dusty road, doubled over as if in pain—though I remember no pain.

Before me stands a woman, dressed all in black. Her face is wrinkled and old, her eyes blue green and cold. She says, "Let that be a lesson to you, you arrogant pig." Then she raises her arms and all in an instant is transformed into a crow and flies away.

I try to take notice of her direction, which I feel is probably important, but almost immediately lose the tiny speck of black in the glare of the sun. Also, I'm distracted by the thought that I have no idea who the woman is, or why she should have said such a thing to me.

More alarming, I realize I have no idea who *I* am.

A young man—that I can tell. I frantically ransack my brain, but no name surfaces. No face, either—my own or anyone else's, except the one I've just seen, the old woman's with the cold eyes. *This is ridiculous,* I think, *I'm...*

But even with this running start I can't finish the thought. No name. I can't even think: I'm so-and-so's son. I feel no connection to anyone or anything before fifteen seconds ago.

My clothes are satin and brocade. I have two rings, one on each hand—one is set with two emeralds; the other is simple gold, in the form of a dragon eating its own tail. I also have a gold clasp for my cloak. *So,* I reason, *I'm a wealthy man.* And, it takes no memory but only common sense to know, wealth means power. But I don't feel powerful, without even having a name.

I look around. The countryside is unfamiliar without being strange. I am on a road, fairly wide and clear. The land is a bit hilly, behind me more so, ahead of me less. Also ahead of me, rising above the tops of the trees, I can make out a distant tower. Much closer is a horse, grazing on the weeds by the edge of the road. I think he must be mine, for he is saddled and bridled, and there is no one else in sight, and what need does a woman who can turn herself into a crow have for a horse?

But I have no name for the horse, any more than I have for myself, and he looks at me warily as I rise to my feet.

"It's all right," I assure him, making soft clucking noises to calm him. "Everything is fine."

Obviously we can both see everything is *not* fine, but he lets me approach, although he watches me with eyes so alarmed the whites show around them.

I can tell that the horse, like the clothing, is expensive. So are the horse's accoutrements. The saddle is soft leather, just worn enough to be broken in and comfortable, not old or scuffed. The saddle-cloth is expensive material and looks brand-new. There are no saddlebags, nothing to tell me who I am or where I'm from.

"Steady," I tell the horse, and I swing up into the saddle. The action seems natural and familiar. I gather I'm accustomed to riding, but there's no further enlightenment. I face the horse in the direction of the tower, which I hope is a castle. Where I hope someone will recognize me.

I imagine someone—there is no face: I'm imagining, not planning—that someone placing a cool cloth on my head. I imagine this person saying, "The poor dear had a nasty spill from the horse, but he'll be fine in the morning."

But I remember the blue-green eyes of the black-clothed woman, and in my heart I know it's not going to be that simple.

The tower does turn out to be part of a castle. The castle overlooks a town. Still, no names come to mind.

I ride through the town gate, and people scurry out of the way of my horse. When I get to the gate of the castle itself, guards standing at either side bow, which might mean they recognize me. Or which might mean my clothes and my horse make me look important enough to warrant polite behavior.

In the courtyard, I dismount and a steward comes and bows. "Good day, sir," he says. "May I announce you?" He gestures for a page to come take the horse.

Somewhat reluctantly, for the horse is my only connection to any past at all, I let go of the reins and watch the boy lead the horse in the direction that must be the stables. "Yes," I tell the senior servant. "Please do."

"Your name, sir?" the steward asks.

I sigh, thinking everything would have been so much simpler if this had turned out to be my home. "Don't you know me?" I ask hopefully. Perhaps he'll take guesses, and one of them will sound familiar.

But the steward just says, apologetically, "I'm afraid your lordship's face is unfamiliar to me." His smile gets just the least bit impatient as he waits.

"I . . ." I say. "I seem to have had a mishap on the road . . ."

"Indeed?" the old servant says, sounding decidedly cooler by now.

"I think I may have been struck on the head," I say, unwilling to share the thought that I seem to have gotten on the wrong side of a woman who can turn herself into a crow.

"How unfortunate," the steward says, his tone bland, but his face disapproving. I can tell, by his face, that people of real quality, such as he is used to dealing with, don't have such things happen to them.

"I was hoping," I admit, "that someone might recognize me."

"I don't," the steward says.

"Perhaps someone else," I suggest.

The steward thinks I am insulting him. "I know everyone who comes and goes at this castle," he tells me.

"But maybe," I insist, "the lord of this castle might know me."

The steward looks me up and down as though I'm a disgrace to my fine clothing. But he doesn't dare turn me away for fear that maybe his lord *would* recognize me, so he says, "The lord and his lady may or may not be in the audience hall this afternoon. You may wait there."

"There was a lady on the road . . ." I say, with a

flash of remembrance of hard eyes, of the swish of fabric as arms are raised....

"Not *our* lady," the steward assures me, and turns his back on me.

I'm so annoyed by his attitude, I call after him, though I know my presence here is dependent on his goodwill, "Once I regain my identity, you'll apologize for your bad manners."

He looks back scornfully. "Doubtful," he says.

All afternoon long I wait with a crowd of other petitioners for the arrival of the castle's lord.

As evening shadows lengthen and the wonderful smells of cooking waft into the audience hall, we are told that the lord will not be seeing us today. Go home. Try again some other day.

I ask to see the steward, but he is not available, either. The servants are very sorry, very polite, but in no time I'm back out in the courtyard, and the castle door shuts in my face.

I find out where the stables are, but my horse is not there. When I admit to the stable master that I'm not a guest at the castle, he tells me that the stables only house the horses of the castle inhabitants and their guests.

"But a boy took my horse away," I protest, "when I first arrived and the steward greeted me."

"Ah," the stable master says, "I know who you are."

My heart starts to beat faster, but he only means that the steward has warned him about me. The horse was originally brought to the stable, he says, but the steward ordered him removed when it was discovered I had no legitimate business at the castle. The horse, the stable master says, is tied up out back behind the smallest stable building, and with that he closes the stable door in my face as firmly as the castle servants closed the castle door in my face.

I am unable to remember who I am or anything else about me, but I am fairly certain I have never had doors shut in my face before.

Going to the back of the building, I find my horse tied to a post, looking disconsolate. His saddle has been removed and is sitting on the ground beside him, but the grooms did not have time to curry him before the steward changed their orders. The horse's healthy coat beneath a layer of road dust shows that he's used to better treatment, and, worse yet, there is no vegetation within reach of his tether.

"Come on, horse," I say, untying him. The area around the castle is all paving stones and packed dirt, so—carrying the saddle—I lead the horse out through the castle gate, through the winding streets of the town, and out the town gate. The smell of all that fine hay and grain just the other side of the stable wall must have been just as frustrating for him as the smell of the castle supper being prepared was for me.

Beyond the town walls there's grass, and the horse is happy with that. We have to wander farther to find a stream, and we both drink from there.

Distantly we hear a bell ringing, and too late I realize it's the town curfew. By the time we get back to the wall, the gates have been shut and locked for the night.

I tie the horse's reins to a tree, then put the saddle on the ground to use as a pillow. This does *not* feel natural and familiar, and I have the feeling this is *not* something I've done before. Another unpleasant first for me.

The night does not bring back any of my lost memories. I try to convince myself that I imagined the old woman with the blue-green eyes, that I really did get struck on the head, and that eventually my memory is bound to return.

But in my heart I know this is not true. In my heart I know that the woman was there, that she was a witch, and that for some reason she has bespelled me.

In the darkest hours I wonder just how far her spell has worked: Has she destroyed my memories, or do I have no memories because previously I did not exist to *have* memories? I think with alarm of all those stories with witches and frogs. *But she didn't call me a frog,* I console myself; *she called me a pig.* Still, while I cannot remember my name, or my family, or my country, there are certain things I know: I know, for one, there is a certain connection between witches and frogs; I know the difference between north, south, east, and west; I know to be embarrassed and humiliated by the way the servants have treated me; I know how to walk on two legs, and that feels natural to me, as does riding a horse and sleeping—if I could—indoors. But anything personal, anything that could lead me to who I am, is gone. And my only hope is that the unknown lord of this unknown castle in this unknown land will somehow miraculously know me.

In the morning, when the town gates open, I pick what grass and leaves I can feel out of my hair and once again approach the castle. There's nothing I can do about the grass stains on my clothes. I use the saddlecloth to rub the horse down, and the horse gives me a look that says he's used to *much* better.

I find the steward again, looking more disapproving than before. Perhaps it's the grass stains. Perhaps it's the horse trailing behind me, as far as the reins will let him get so that it appears even *he* doesn't want to be associated with me. Perhaps the steward is worried that I plan to bring the horse with me into the audience hall.

When I ask the steward what the chances are of seeing the lord today, he snorts and says it's Sunday. No audiences on Sunday.

By now I'm so hungry I think: *If the horse gives me any trouble, I'll eat him.* But I know I won't. He may well be my only way to get home.

I find one of the young boys who helps in the stables. First I throw myself on his mercy, but he's pitiless. Then I offer him my ring with the emeralds. One of the things I have no memory of, no sense for, is money. Either I've never had money, or—more likely—I've never not had enough money. I can tell, though, by the glint in the young page's eyes, what a good bargain he's struck. A gold ring with two emeralds for a stall big enough for my horse and—since I have no better choice—myself to stay in until after I've been seen by the lord of the castle. The ring pays for oats and water for the horse, what food the boy can smuggle from the kitchen for me, the use of a currycomb so I can groom the horse, and the boy's secrecy, because I suspect if the steward or the stable master knew, they'd throw us right out.

True to his word, the boy keeps me fed with hard cheese and harder bread. This diet does nothing to improve my memory.

After three days the lord finally comes to the audience hall to speak to the petitioners, but there isn't time for him to deal with each of us, and he leaves without seeing me.

The fourth day the lord returns. I realize I'm getting more and more disreputable-looking as I sleep in my clothes, and straw gets ground into my hair, and I pick up the scent of the stables. The servants must be getting alarmed by my continuing presence, for as the lord starts to leave, once again without glancing at me, I see the steward whisper to him. The lord looks up, over the heads of the bowing crowd, and directly at me.

I take a step forward.

The lord leans down to whisper to the steward, shaking his head.

He doesn't know me.

After all this, he doesn't know me.

The lord leaves, the crowd disperses, and the steward comes up to me and smirks, "Ready for your apology?"

He has two younger, burlier servants with him, and they take hold of my arms and fling me out the door.

When I pick myself up, I find my young stable boy watching me. He's holding on to the reins of my horse, and my saddle is flung over the horse's back, though it's not fastened. The boy says, "The stable master found your horse and says you have to leave."

As I take the reins, the boy whispers to me, "For

your other ring, I could find another place for you."

I shake my head, knowing I cannot afford his prices.

Heading for the castle gate, I pass the stable master. "It's a good horse, though," he calls out to me. "Are you willing to sell him?"

I shake my head, for the horse is my ride home.

I go out through the castle gate and into the town itself. But I stop short of leaving the town. What should I do? I know I'm lost; but when someone is lost, it's best to stay in one place, lest you accidentally elude anyone searching for you.

Is there anyone searching for me?

I could go from town to town, one step ahead of my would-be rescuers. And quickly run through all my possessions and be no better off. I decide to stay in this town and hope that there *is* someone missing me, trying to find me.

Looking from the horse and his saddle to my dragon ring, to the gold sunburst pin that holds my cloak, I notice how shabby my once-fine clothes are beginning to appear. They won't last long, so they're what I'll start with. I begin to search for someone who'll buy the clothes off my back—trade sturdiness for finery and hopefully give me a few extra coins in the bargain so I can eat.

With the money I get for trading my clothes and selling my pin, I can afford a week's meals and lodgings for myself and a stall for my horse in the stable of a small inn. Every day I take the horse out to graze on the grass outside the town walls, so I don't have to use up my small amount of money to buy food for him.

I go around the town, talking to people, hungry for names. Nothing sounds familiar. Nobody looks familiar to me. And I look familiar to no one.

The dragon emblem on my ring seems to be just a decoration—it means nothing to anyone. So, after the week, I offer the ring to the owner of the inn. He says it will buy me two more weeks' lodging. I bargain with him. I say: "Three weeks' worth of food, and I'll stay in the stable with the horse."

The innkeeper is not pleased with the arrangement, but finally he agrees. *I'm* not happy with the arrangement, for the stalls are much smaller than at the castle's stables, and I'll be lucky if I don't get stepped on. Still, I'm assuming that in three weeks I'm bound to remember or find out *some*thing about my past.

But after three weeks I have to approach the innkeeper with yet another bargain. "I'll work for my keep," I offer, "mine and the horse's."

The innkeeper lifts up my hand, which is soft and white compared to his. "Never done a day's work in your life," he snorts.

I don't remember, one way or the other, but my hands say he is right.

"I can learn," I tell him.

The innkeeper raises his eyes to the heavens and shakes his head, but he agrees.

My job is to muck out the stable twice every day. In addition, I have to keep the inn clean, too, the common room and the guest rooms. My hands are blistered and my muscles are sore, but I get to eat all the leftovers I can scrape from customers' plates.

Unfortunately, all this work leaves little time for taking my horse out to graze, and meanwhile the weather is beginning to turn colder. Soon there will be no foraging. First I sell the saddle, telling myself that once I find out where home is I can ride there without a saddle. With the money I get from selling it, I buy enough oats to make the horse happy again. For a time.

But then that runs out, and I see he's getting skinnier and skinnier. Eventually I realize I have to sell him soon, or the castle's stable master won't want him.

"I'm sorry, horse," I whisper. I still don't remember his name, and I have no way of knowing how fond of him I was before. Now he is the only thing I have left to connect me to the furthest back I can remember: the day on the road with the blue-green-eyed witch.

The stable master buys the horse, with much grumbling and shaking of his head over the horse's sad state. After all we've been through together—

maybe *because of* all we've been through—the horse doesn't look sorry to leave me.

As I walk through the town, I give one of my coins to the man with the withered hand who stands on the same street corner every day, begging. It isn't that I have money to spare, but I recognize that this may well be where I end up next.

At the inn the innkeeper tells me that he's sorry—I've been a better worker than he ever imagined—but his nephew has arrived from the country, looking for a job, and the innkeeper has given him mine.

It's been so long since I've been clean, or comfortable, or well fed, I'm desperate enough to be willing to spend some of my money from the sale of my horse to take a room. But when I reach into my pocket, I find nothing there but a hole.

I leave, so that the innkeeper doesn't have to throw me out, the way the castle steward threw me out.

I walk down the street, wondering if I should beg my coin back from the beggar. From behind me, I hear the clatter of horses' hooves on the street. I press against the wall to get out of the way—the lord and lady of the castle and their friends are always tearing through the streets on their fast mounts, careless of the poor folk who have to scurry out of their way.

The riders, two men, have to slow down to take the corner. I look to see if either of the horses is mine, but neither is. I keep walking, the only way to stay warm, but one of the men pulls his horse to a stop; and the second man stops, also, to avoid colliding with him.

"Your Highness?" a voice says.

I look up and around, and it's the first man, and he's looking at me.

"Is it you?" he asks in sick amazement.

"I don't know," I have to admit. "Is it?"

He leaps from his horse for a closer look, then practically kneels, he bows so low.

"Our long-lost prince, found at last," he proclaims to any of the town's inhabitants who might be wondering. He whips off his cloak and puts it around me. "Oh, well met, sir," he exclaims with such joy it nearly breaks my heart.

He orders the younger man with him to get off his horse. "Help His Highness up," he says, "and you walk along behind."

Belatedly the younger man scrambles off his horse, and he actually *does* kneel on the cobblestones.

"How far to home?" I ask.

"Two weeks' journey," the older man tells me.

I know how sore my feet have been since I sold my fine boots with the rest of my clothing, and I can't subject this poor young squire to walking for two weeks. "We can ride together," I say, which makes his eyes go wide in amazement.

And so we do.

I learn my name, which does not sound familiar, and I learn that I have a father and mother who have been frantic concerning my whereabouts, and there is a princess to whom I am betrothed— foreign born but lovely, I'm assured—and none of their names sound familiar, either. And when we finally reach my ancestral lands, nothing *looks* familiar.

The man who found me—one of many such searchers, he informs me—sends word ahead that I have been found, but that my memory has been lost. We enter the courtyard to my own castle— which looks less familiar to me than the castle in the town where I stayed. I return to the sound of trumpets blaring and men cheering and maid- ens throwing flower petals out the windows to greet me.

A gray-bearded man and a plump woman are standing by the fountain, and before the horses even stop, the woman is rushing forward, crying out, "Oh, my poor, sweet baby."

"Mother," I say, which seems a fairly safe guess, and she throws her arms around me, then turns to the crowd and says, triumphantly, defiantly, "See? He *does* remember."

But I don't.

I have to take other people's word for who I know, and who I like, and what I did as a boy, and what my interests are, and that I love my parents, and that I'm happy with my betrothal to the princess.

They tell me I'm calmer than I ever was before, and more patient, and kinder. Which sound like compliments, until I think about it. When I point this out, everybody laughs and says, *No, no, but we mean it—we loved you before, but you're gentler and more considerate since your adventure.*

Whatever my adventure was.

Which is the one thing none of them knows, either.

And *nothing* seems familiar.

Except, sometimes, when I look at the princess I'm to marry, I find her looking at me with an expression that's almost familiar, watching carefully, appraisingly, and her eyes are cool blue green, and that's something I don't want to think about at all.

WITCH-HUNT

Lyssa saw her first witch trial and public burning when she was six years old. But it wasn't until she was ten that she learned the witch-hunters were after her and her parents. And it wasn't until she was thirteen that the witch-hunters finally tracked her family down.

It was a quiet summer evening. Her father, who owned and worked the same land his father had cleared and plowed before him, was outside for one final after-dinner check on the animals before coming in for the night. Lyssa and her mother were at the kitchen table, kneading and forming dough, which they would leave to rise overnight.

Lyssa heard a sound near the door that she thought was her father cleaning off his boots before coming in.

But her father didn't come through the door.

Lyssa had just long enough to wonder what was delaying him. Then the door burst open with a crunching of wood and a crash. And a voice was shouting at them not to move, don't try anything, don't make a bad situation worse. White-garbed witch-hunters rushed into the kitchen—five of them ... no, six ... no, eight—men and women alike, their heavy, muddy boots stomping across the kitchen floor that Lyssa's father wasn't allowed to walk on except with stockinged feet.

Before Lyssa could move—before what she was seeing had fully registered—her mother grabbed hold of her, dough-covered fingers digging into her shoulders, trying to put herself between Lyssa and the witch-hunters.

"Don't—" her mother started, but by then the witch-hunters were on them, and they yanked them apart.

There was movement from behind, more witch-hunters, who had come in through the back of the house. "Satanic bibles," one of those said. He was wearing thick leather gloves that reached almost to his elbows, as though the very touch of the books would contaminate him. He let the books drop to the floor. Three of them. Hers. Which meant the man had been in her room, looking through her things, had lifted the mattress off her bed. It must be the most common of hiding places, that he had found it so quickly. She could hear someone still rummaging through her parents' room. Already the witch-hunters had her mother's hands bound behind her back. "The child?" someone asked.

It was the first time Lyssa was glad to look younger than she was, for the witch-hunter in charge hesitated, then shook his head *no*.

And then there was another flurry of activity by the front door, and another witch-hunter entered.

Any hope of her parents being able to talk their way out of this situation, of finding a means to escape—any hope sank with the realization that the newcomer was Norah Raybournne, the woman known as the Witch-Hunter General. She had no such title, of course, only a relentless enthusiasm to seek out God's enemies, and a gift for leadership. It was said Norah Raybournne was well aware of the name the people had given her and did not object to it.

"So..." the Witch-Hunter General said softly, walking around the room, as though to study Lyssa and her mother from different angles. She made a wide circle, lest the hem of her white gown pass over the books her people had found in Lyssa's bed. "So..." Her hair was gray, and she wore it in a simple braid that hung halfway down her back. There was nothing soft, nothing frivolous about her. She was a tall woman, and when she stopped in front of Lyssa, Lyssa found herself at eye level to the heavy gold cross the Witch-Hunter General wore low on her chest—a cross engraved with an eye, the witch-hunters' symbol, to indicate ever-vigilance.

Not ungently, the Witch-Hunter General took hold of Lyssa's chin, forcing her head back and her gaze—unless she closed her eyes—up. Her touch was dry and cool. *Like a snake,* Lyssa thought.

As though she could read Lyssa's thought through her eyes, the Witch-Hunter General shook her head. "Pitiful," she said. Not letting go of Lyssa, she shifted her attention to Lyssa's mother. "Pitiful child of Satan. How could you corrupt her like this?"

Instead of answering, Lyssa's mother demanded, "Where's my husband?"

Neither did the Witch-Hunter General answer. She said, "You and your husband both have much to answer for." Her eyes came to rest on Lyssa once again. "Perhaps it's not too late for the little one," she said, "with fit parents. Though I much doubt it."

Lyssa jerked her face away. She could imagine what *fit parents* meant to witch-hunters.

"Burn the house," the Witch-Hunter General ordered.

Lyssa's mother kicked the shin of the witch-hunter standing nearest her. Startled, the woman cried out, drawing everyone's attention. Even the Witch-Hunter General.

Fit parents, Lyssa thought. Once the witch-hunters handed her over to her new *fit parents,* she'd be trapped for life—or until, if ever, she could convince them she'd forgotten her witchly ways. If she had the power the witch-hunters were so afraid of, she'd use it. But her only chance—her parents' only chance—was for her to run.

And run she did, heading for the back of the house.

Except that she'd forgotten the witch-hunter with the gloves.

He lunged at her, and she dodged, but she was just the tiniest bit too slow. His bulky hand was about to close around her arm when her foot came down on the pile of books on the floor. The top volume slid forward while the other two stayed where they were, and Lyssa all unintentionally dropped below the grasp of the man's hand.

Lyssa grabbed one of the books and, in one fluid motion she'd never have accomplished if she'd stopped to think about it, brought the edge hard against his knee. By luck, she struck just the right spot, and his leg buckled.

And then she was on her feet, still holding the book, and running past her parents' room. The witch-hunter who'd been searching there made a rush for her, but she eluded that one's grasp also and made it into her room. She leapt over her possessions, which had been dumped unceremoniously onto the floor, and scrambled through the open window.

She heard shouting. Witch-hunters were following, some coming the way she had, others—who must have been in the front guarding her father—circling around the outside of the house.

Drawn by the commotion of the witch-hunters, neighbors had gathered. Simple farmers for the most part. People she'd known all her life. Some few might be sympathetic, but there was no being sure if or who. Lyssa headed off into the woods. Branches raked at her hair and arms. She knew she was leaving a trail anyone could follow, but there was no time for cleverness. She had to get some distance ahead of them, then she could try back-tracking or crossing the stream or climbing a tree and jumping squirrel-like to another—tricks she'd learned from reading Satanic bibles.

Her dress snagged on a branch, pulling her up short. She tugged, ripping the fabric, and went skittering down a bank, closer to the stream than she had expected. Her books had taught her about walking in the water, so as not to leave telltale impressions of her passing. But now that she was here, she saw that going upstream would bring her rapidly out into the open, and downstream was impassable because of a fallen tree, which would take too long to climb over, or around, or under.

Still clutching the book, unwilling to lose her

last tie to her parents, she splashed through the unexpectedly chilly stream and scrambled up the other side, leaving distinctly fresh gashes in the muddy bank where her feet slipped.

Though it was dusk, dark was a long time coming on summer nights, and suddenly, behind her, she heard the baying of the witch-hunters' dogs, trained trackers. There would be no gathering of fallen branches and last year's leaves to hide beneath.

Lyssa pressed her hand to her aching side and zig-zagged through the woods. She came to the stream yet again, pursuit still close enough to hear. Upstream was the same felled tree that had blocked her before. Or downstream, which the witch-hunters would know was the only way she could go without running into those on the far bank.

She splashed noisily. The water came up to her knees, dragging at her, making speed impossible. And then the ground was no longer where it should be. She pitched forward, almost dropping the book, as the water closed in over her head. But as soon as she stopped panicking, she found she was able to stand after all, with the water only to her waist. Still sputtering, she waded out on the side where her house was, hoping her pursuers wouldn't look for her this close to home.

If only she could elude them till dark, she

thought. Then she could cut across the field unseen, make her way to her aunt's house. Surely her aunt would protect her for family's sake.

But suddenly a bright light flashed out of the dimness, blinding her. A loud voice called out, "Escape is impossible."

Lyssa spun around to retrace her steps. But after that incredible brightness, she could make out nothing but shadows. Hands grabbed her, took hold of her arms, turned her back in the direction of that awful light. Somebody shouted an order, and the light went out. Lyssa was marched in the direction of the voices and the dogs by two sure-footed witch-hunters. The books were full of people using spells to get out of situations just like this, but there was nothing Lyssa could do.

They reached her backyard in minutes. Her escape attempt had been pathetic. Her parents had already been taken away. She might never see them again.

The Witch-Hunter General stepped forward from the brightly lighted front lawn. Shaking her head, she wrenched the sodden book from Lyssa's hand. *No gloves for her,* Lyssa noted. She wished the book *did* have some special power. She wished the Witch-Hunter General's hand would fall off.

But of course it didn't.

———

Norah Raybournne, representative of Citizens for a Better Community, watched as the black-and-white police car rounded the curve of the driveway, taking away the evil child. Norah never referred to herself as a witch-hunter, though she rather liked the name. She performed a valuable and sometimes dangerous service, and the fact that the people she pursued called her witch-hunter provided what any straight-thinking person would find an unsettling insight into their psyches.

She dropped the Satanic bible in a plastic bag, not because she was afraid of being contaminated, but because it was dripping. It would have to be dried out before it could be destroyed at one of the public burnings. She had seen this particular version before anyway and didn't need to inspect it. *So sad*, she thought. How could people *do* that? Intentionally pervert their own child, exposing her to Satan's influence so that she would never—Norah was sure of it—be fit for anything besides life in a federal penitentiary, where she wouldn't be able to spread her evil influence to others.

The dispenser of hand wipes that she kept under the dashboard was empty, so Norah wiped her hands on her grandson's football jersey, which would be easier to launder than her uniform. Then she opened the case of her computer to catalog the Satanic bible. What was the appeal, she wondered with contempt, of a book whose only purpose was to deceive?

Norah scrolled down the checklist to the section for children. The biggie, of course, was Unauthorized Miracles (a.k.a. Magic), *subsection* Wishes Fulfilled by an Agency Other Than God (Implication: SATAN).

She also put checks by:

—Grossly Unlifelike Illustrations, Giving Children a Distorted Sense of Aesthetics So That They Become Dissatisfied with Their Own Appearance.

—Women as Victims.

—Inaccurate Historical Representation That May Confuse.

—Unrealistic Depiction of Animals That May Cause Disappointment and/or Physical Harm to Children Expecting Real Animals to Behave in Like Manner.

—Unfair and Demeaning Stereotypes of Nontraditional Nuclear Family Units.

—Fulfillment of Unreal Expectations, Leading Children to a Life of Disappointment and Self-Recrimination.

Norah Raybournne snapped shut the lid of the computer and started the car. She shuddered at the thought of the book beside her, even though she wasn't a superstitious woman, even though she knew it couldn't harm her unless she let it.

Cinderella.

It was one of the worst, and she wouldn't rest easy till she had destroyed every copy.

CYPRESS SWAMP GRANNY

MARIETTA SAT ON THE VERANDA fanning herself, because there's nothing hotter and stickier than August in New Orleans, and indoors wouldn't even be bearable till evening. "The trouble is," she complained, "all the best boys went off to that stupid war, and what came back was worse than what stayed."

"Hush!" Mama gave a frantic look to Papa, snoring one chair over; for Papa was one of those who had gone, and he had lost a foot to an artillery barrage at the first battle of Manassas, which the Yankees called Bull Run.

Marietta waved her fan dismissively. It was one thing for Papa to have to walk with a cane. It was quite another matter to have boys Marietta was supposed to *dance* with come back from the war with arms and legs missing, or with awful scars, or—

worst yet—like Billy Renfrew, who looked as fine as ever but now just sat there, his eyes focused on something nobody else could see; and occasionally his mother had to get out a handkerchief and wipe the drool from his chin.

"It just isn't fair," Marietta insisted.

"I swear"—Mama leaned back in her chair—"sometimes you're the most heartless child I know."

"Seventeen is not a child," said Marietta. "And all I'm saying is, it's a sad day when Louisa Beth Eldridge's family is giving a ball in one week's time, and the most eligible bachelor around is Will Stottle, with his too-narrow shoulders and his too-wide behind."

Mama patted Marietta's arm sympathetically. "Not," Mama pointed out, "of course, that Will Stottle is eligible anymore. He and your cousin Violet *have* formalized their engagement."

"Oh, Mother!" Marietta cried in exasperation. She shoved back her chair, with a scraping of wood on wood.

—just as young Ceecee, carrying a tray with glasses of tea, eased open the front door.

The chair hit the door, the door hit the tray—and tray, pitcher, and glasses crashed to the floor.

Mama cried out, brushing at the hem of her gown.

Papa snorted in his sleep but didn't wake up.

Ceecee, eight years old and unsure whether to curtsy and apologize first, or cry, or pick up the broken glass, or mop up the spreading puddle of tea, bobbed and wavered, trying to accomplish all at once.

Marietta fought the inclination to kick her, lest some bleeding-heart Yankee reconstructionist complain that they were mistreating the black help who had chosen to remain—at a *salary*, no less. Would anyone have believed such a thing just a few years back?

"This is unbearable!" Marietta cried, sweeping past Ceecee, who'd crouched to clean up the mess she had made. Ceecee leaned back to avoid the swing of Marietta's hem, lost her balance, and sat down heavily in the wetness.

Marietta ran down the veranda stairs and across the front lawn. At the very first, the breeze of running blew her hair off her face, which felt good. But after a short distance her clothes were clinging to her as though she had taken them damp off the line. She stopped running but didn't turn back.

The war hadn't ruined the DuChamps family, as it had ruined so many others. Their property had more or less survived intact—excepting the loss of the slaves, of course. But time was they could afford to go someplace cool for August, and that was certainly one more change for the worse.

On the hard-worn dirt path that led down to the

river road, Marietta heard the light pitter-pat of Ceecee's bare feet.

"Missus says to go with you," Ceecee said. "See you don't get into trouble."

"Trouble?" Marietta shouted, though Mama would have said shouting wasn't refined. "*Trouble?* There's nothing to *do*."

"When I don't have nothing special to do," Ceecee said, "or when I'm troubled, I go visit my granny Orilla."

Marietta continued walking, though she had no destination in mind. Paris would have been nice. Natchez acceptable.

Ceecee came skipping after her. "Granny Orilla knows cures and curses—all kinds of spells—and she knows dreams—"

Marietta stopped so quickly that Ceecee almost collided with her. "What are you talking about?" she demanded.

"When my sister was afraid that her man was going to leave her, Granny Orilla gave her a root to put under his pillow, and he hasn't gone wandering since."

"A *root*?" Marietta repeated scornfully.

"White folk come to her, too, sometime," Ceecee said. "Remember how hard Missus Nattie wanted a baby, and she couldn't have none? Granny made a remedy for her she had to rub on her belly every night for six nights, and the seventh night she drank down what was left, and before the hibiscus bloomed—"

"Quiet," Marietta commanded, for everyone knew Nathalie Nye had had twin boys last year, after years of trying. "Where is this granny of yours?" she asked, for she had nothing better to do.

"Lives down by the cypress swamp," Ceecee said.

"Of course she does." Marietta sighed. "Lead the way."

The closer Marietta and Ceecee got to the swamp, the louder the insects whined and buzzed, sounding fierce enough to carry off small children. Granny Orilla's shack was nestled among moss-draped oaks.

"Granny Orilla!" Ceecee hollered shrilly, startling the chickens out from under the porch. "Granny Orilla!"

The old, skinny woman who came out of the cabin, leaning heavily on a hickory stick cane, was Creole—a mix: Most likely her daddy had been a plantation owner with an eye for the pretty slaves. This woman was not pretty, or at least she hadn't been in ages. Her hair—what she had left—was perfectly white.

"Ceecee, honey!" she crowed.

Ugly old thing, Marietta thought as girl and woman hugged.

"This is Miss Marietta," Ceecee said, "come to see you."

"How kind of you to visit," the woman Orilla said, too polite—sarcastic, even—as though she had read Marietta's thoughts on her face.

Ceecee dragged on her grandmother's arm, bringing her closer. "I was telling her about things you done, like for Missus Nattie," Ceecee said, "and she wanted to meet you."

Quick, before Marietta knew what was happening, Orilla laid her hand on Marietta's belly. "No luck making babies?" she asked.

Marietta slapped the bony hand away. "Uppity old witch," she said. "Time was, I could have had you whipped for your insolence."

Orilla smiled a swamp creature's smile. "Times change," she answered.

Trying to make peace, Ceecee told Orilla, "She don't need help with babies. She don't even have a man."

Orilla continued to smile, as though the fault lay somehow with *Marietta* rather than with the war taking all the best boys away. "You looking to win one man special," she asked, "or any man?"

Marietta opened her mouth to protest, but then realized that *was* why she'd come. "Will Stottle," she answered.

She was aware of Ceecee gaping at her. "But that's Miss Violet's beau," the child said.

Orilla's dark eyes shifted from Marietta to Ceecee, back to Marietta.

"Will Stottle," Marietta repeated. "Ceecee says you've got some sort of root, or something?"

The smile widened. Orilla's teeth were yellow from age and looked too big for her shrunken, wrinkled face, giving her a slightly horsey appearance, though Marietta estimated there was more of crocodile than horse in Orilla's smile. "Oh, there's roots and there's herbs," the old woman said, "each with its own purpose. Let me see your hand."

She ran her callused finger along the lines that crossed Marietta's palm. *"Mmm-mmm-MMMM,"* she said, shaking her head disapprovingly.

Marietta snatched her hand away.

Orilla made her eyes go all wide and spooky. "I see you burning bright with the fire of passion," she said. "I see you driving that poor boy mad with the wanting of you."

"But only with your help?" Marietta guessed, smirking.

Orilla let her eyes return to normal. "Girl like you should be satisfied with what you got. You should enjoy the sweet life the Lord give you while you can."

"I don't want your *advice*," Marietta said. "I want one of your potions. Or a root. Or an herb." She gave her own crocodile smile. "Or can't you do it?"

"There's a price," Orilla told her. "I'll require a year from your life."

"You expect *me* to work for *you* for a year? For Will *Stottle*?"

"Nothing to do with work, honey," Orilla said. "Not a year of your time. A year of your life. I'll take it off the end, where you're least likely to miss it, to add on to mine."

"Crazy old witch," Marietta said. "How, exactly, do you plan to collect this year?"

"By taking your hand, and you wishing it onto me."

Marietta looked at Ceecee, wondering what the catch was, what the two of them were up to. But she couldn't read anything on Ceecee's face. "Taken a lot of years from people, have you?" Marietta asked, flipping her hand, palm up, practically in Orilla's face. Orilla looked seventy or eighty.

"Oh no." Orilla grinned. "This is something new I just learned." She rubbed a finger along the line that started between Marietta's thumb and forefinger and ran down to the wrist.

*Some*thing happened—a pain similar to hitting her elbow in just the wrong place.

Marietta snatched her hand back.

"Sorry," Orilla said. "Thank you." She had her hand clasped, as though to hold on tight to the year she seemed to believe she had taken.

What have I done? Marietta thought, suddenly afraid.

"It's only a year," Ceecee reassured her.

Marietta rubbed her hand, although, really, it had stopped hurting already. "What good's a year?" she taunted. Orilla *still* looked seventy or eighty.

"I can take this one year of yours"—Orilla held up her fist—"and stretch it out to ten years for me. Come." She gestured for Marietta to follow her into her cabin.

Which was probably as filthy as the slave shacks had ever been, and just as likely to fall down. "I'll wait here," Marietta said.

Orilla gave her awful smile, and she and Ceecee went indoors, leaving Marietta with the chickens.

Crazy old witch, Marietta thought again. Probably Orilla'd scratched her fingernail along Marietta's palm to cause that painful tingle, that old trickster. There was no mark, but Marietta found her cheeks burning at the thought of how frightened she'd momentarily been. A year, indeed!

But then the two of them came out, Ceecee skipping merrily, Orilla carrying a tiny burlap bag. "You sure this Will Stottle is the man you want?" Orilla asked. "Because this is a powerful remedy. And it only works the once."

"It only needs to work once," Marietta said. She didn't like the smile Orilla gave her at that.

"With the lights out and your eyes closed, go to

sleep tonight thinking of your man," Orilla instructed. "Hold on to this here bag all night long.
In the morning, you take the hand you held on to
that bag with, and you make sure the first person
you touch is him, skin to skin, without touching
nobody in between."

Marietta sniffed the bag. Nothing foul, in any
case. "Come along, Ceecee," she said, and headed
back home without a thank-you or good-bye.

The next afternoon, Marietta paid a call on her
cousin Violet. As she'd expected, Will Stottle was
there.

Marietta kissed Violet's cheek. "Being in love
suits you," she told Violet, not meaning a word of
it. "You look lovely."

She let the old swamp granny's burlap bag drop
from her hand into the silk purse that dangled from
the same wrist. *All night long,* the old witch had said.
Marietta had held the bag all morning, too, just to
make sure. She clasped Will's hand in both of hers.
"And, my, don't you look dashing! You make such
a handsome couple."

"Well, thank you," Will said, not letting go of
her hand.

In his eyes, Marietta saw a flicker of something
that could have been a moment's surprise.

It worked, she thought in amazement, as Will
continued to hold her hands and stare and stare as

though he couldn't get enough of her. She hadn't quite believed it *could*, but Will was obviously having trouble remembering how to breathe.

"Well," Violet said in a fluttery voice after several—long—moments of the two of them looking deeply into each other's eyes, "how kind of you to visit, Marietta." She linked her arm around Will's, and he never even glanced at her.

"I came to let you know," Marietta said in a breathy voice, still gazing wistfully at Will, "if there's anything at all you want, you should be sure to just ask."

"Isn't that sweet?" Violet said. Good-natured as a lop-eared pup, and about as intelligent, even she could see that something was wrong. "Thank you," she said. "You're very kind." Then: "Will, I'm sure Marietta has other errands to run today, and we really shouldn't keep her any longer." She shook his arm. *"Will."*

Marietta finally pulled her hands from Will's, first the left, then the right, that which had held Orilla's bag. She said, "You must come to visit me."

"Yes," Will agreed, on a long, drawn-out sigh.

"Yes," Violet said, much more shortly.

Outside, Marietta had just barely gotten her sun parasol up when Will burst out of the door. "May I join you?" he called after her.

Marietta smiled, knowing she'd won.

———

Whether the problem was that Will Stottle wasn't a man of strong character to begin with, or that Marietta had held on to Granny Orilla's magical remedy bag too long, Will's single-minded devotion quickly plummeted from flattering to annoying to embarrassing to downright burdensome. He was always there. Always. At her side. Trying to take hold of her elbow. Protesting his undying love.

The night of the Eldridges' ball, Marietta was relieved that Louisa Beth's family had banned Will Stottle because of the scandalous way he had behaved toward Violet.

"Who is that gorgeous man?" she asked Louisa Beth, spying across the room a man who had broad shoulders and a fine behind.

"Daniel Clarke," Louisa Beth said. "He's a business acquaintance of Daddy's. He is—you will kindly pardon the expression—a Yankee—but he's quite charming in spite of it. He's not only handsome, he's almost shamefully rich." Louisa Beth struck her playfully with her fan. "I'll introduce you if you promise not to drive him to distraction, the way you did with poor Will."

Marietta laughed innocently. She had threatened to beat Ceecee senseless—emancipation or not—if she ever said anything about her going to visit Granny Orilla. Everyone assumed the fault was Will's. And it *was* Will's fault, Marietta reasoned. It was one thing to love someone. It was quite another to act the fool.

She followed Louisa Beth around the fringe of the dancing. Close up, the Yankee looked even better than he had from across the room.

"Miss Marietta DuChamps," Louisa Beth said, "may I please present Mr. Daniel Clarke of Pennsylvania. Don't let his youth fool you, Marietta, my dear. Mr. Clarke is a leader of industry *and* banking who now wants to expand his sphere of influence to farming, too."

"How fascinating," Marietta purred, fluttering her eyelashes.

But try as hard as she could to give the impression that she hung on his every word, that she lived only to hear him speak, after a few polite pleasantries, Daniel Clarke let himself get distracted by somebody's mother.

Marietta tried again later that night, when everybody went outside to enjoy the cool of the garden. She even managed to sit down next to him, though she practically had to knock Louisa Beth off the bench. But she could tell he'd already forgotten meeting her, not two hours earlier. Before she could reacquaint him with herself, Will Stottle came crashing through the bougainvillea, begging to be allowed to sit at her feet.

It was obviously time to go home.

———

The next morning, Marietta had Ceecee once more lead her to Granny Orilla's cabin in the cypress swamp.

They found Orilla crawling out from under the porch, gathering the chickens' eggs into a basket. She didn't have her cane with her—not that it would have been much use under the porch.

Did she look younger? Orilla wore a kerchief today, which hid her hair, so Marietta couldn't be sure. Slaves looked old fast, backs bending under constant labor, faces creased by worry. Emancipation didn't cure that. Though Orilla's magic had obviously worked with Will, this business of taking away a year and changing it to ten was harder to believe.

"So, Missy," Orilla greeted her. "How'd my remedy work?"

"Not very well," Marietta said.

"Too well," Ceecee corrected, and knew enough to duck.

"Will Stottle is making a nuisance of himself," Marietta explained. "He won't be put off."

"Week after a love remedy?" Orilla snorted. "I should hope not."

"Make me up a new bag," Marietta said. "Not quite so strong. For a different man, by the name of Daniel Clarke."

Orilla shook her head. "Won't work. I *told* you that. Love remedy only works but the once. Be happy with what you got, sugar. Take things one at a time, each in its own time. No need you have to have a man this very instant."

"I'm willing to pay," Marietta insisted. She'd never heard of somebody refusing to be paid.

But Orilla was still shaking her head.

"If you can't sell me another love potion, sell me something else."

"Like what?" Orilla asked.

Marietta remembered seeing Daniel Clarke talking and laughing with Louisa Beth Eldridge and with Daphne Winslowe and with Dolores Montac. "Make me beautiful."

"All seventeen-year-olds is beautiful," Orilla said. Then, with unexpected kindness, she added, "You're a fine-looking girl."

"I want hair the same golden color as Louisa Beth's. And I want a long, straight nose like Daphne's, and a teeny-tiny waist like Dolores's."

"Those aren't things that matter at all," Orilla said, but she stepped forward. "Hardly worth a year."

Marietta held out her hand.

Shaking her head, no longer giving her swamp-creature smile, Orilla took Marietta's hand and ran a finger over the palm, causing another shiver of pain.

Afterward, she brought out another tiny burlap bag. "Tonight, steep this in a kettleful of hot water until the water boils down to one cupful. Then set the cup to cool where the moonlight is shining on it. Once it's cool enough, drink it all down without taking any breaths in between. And all the while you're drinking, you think on the features you be wanting."

Marietta snatched the bag away, disappointed that she had to wait until the night. "Come, Ceecee," she said.

Still, the bag was a success. By morning, Marietta's hair had lengthened, lightened, thickened, and curled. Her waist curved in nice and tight, and her breasts curved out, and her nose was straight and narrow.

She told her mother—who interrupted to say she looked especially lovely that morning—that she needed to go to Oakridge to thank the Eldridges for the delightful time she'd had at the ball. She didn't mention that she hoped to interrupt the Eldridge family—including their houseguest, Mr. Daniel Clarke—at their breakfast.

Papa rode with her in case Will Stottle should be loitering about the river road, which he was. Papa gave him a stern talking-to, which Marietta guessed did no good at all.

At Oakridge the Eldridges invited Marietta and Papa to join them for breakfast on the veranda. Marietta even managed to squeeze herself between

Daniel and Louisa Beth. Louisa Beth's mother—bless her soul!—commented on how Marietta's gown really suited her figure, and how the color brought out the golden highlights in her hair.

"A beauty," Mr. Eldridge agreed, as Marietta ducked her head shyly, so that her hair would catch the sparkle of the early morning sun. "It's no wonder young Will Stottle is besotted of her."

"Ah," Daniel said, "the young man who had to be forcefully ejected from the ball." He looked at her, Marietta thought, with new appreciation.

"The boy is such a fool," she said.

Daniel raised his eyebrows coolly. "It's difficult to be so young, and so in love."

"Surely, sir," Marietta protested, "you don't excuse his bad manners?"

"I don't excuse anyone's bad manners," Daniel answered. "I simply point out that youthful exuberance is sometimes its own punishment."

"Yes," Louisa Beth said, so solemnly that everyone laughed, and Louisa Beth blushed prettily.

Marietta pouted and plotted.

"The problem is," Marietta told Orilla—who was gray haired but definitely younger than last time—"the Eldridges are rich, and we're only well off."

"A man who cares that much for money," Orilla said, "ain't worth having."

"That's none of your business," Marietta snapped.

"Course it ain't." Orilla was wearing that crocodile smile of hers again. Her teeth gleamed white and strong.

Marietta had found her own way this time, and she was glad Ceecee wasn't here to pick up any of her grandmother's sass.

Orilla, who'd been scrabbling around in her herb garden, wiped her hands on her apron. "Make-money remedies are dangerous," she warned. "A love remedy, a beauty remedy—that's just giving what's already there a nudge. *Money*'s got to come from somewhere. Can't say for certain"—Orilla shook her head—"but lots of time, money comes from somebody else's misfortune—'specially money that comes fast, like you want it." When Marietta didn't answer, she added, "Like maybe somebody dying."

"Are you saying my parents might die?" Marietta asked.

"Not if I make the spell be for money coming into your house," Orilla said. "But other people."

"Then do it." Marietta held her hand out.

"Such a sweet child," Orilla said.

Burying Orilla's bag at midnight was worth the blisters, and the worry she caused Papa—who was sure that moles had invaded the front walk during the night—for the very next morning, as they left Saint Louis Cathedral after mass, a young boy came up to them carrying a big, thick envelope. "Message for Miss Marietta DuChamps from Mr. Will Stottle," the boy announced.

Her parents groaned.

People around them tittered.

But there was no sign of Will, and Orilla had said that bespelled money could come from unexpected directions, so Marietta took the envelope. There was a letter.

> *My dearest Marietta, my love, my reason for living, awakener of my soul, enkindler of my heart, my truest—*

Marietta started skipping words and phrases, aware that the church crowd had not dispersed but was discreetly waiting in the square to see what this was all about. On the third page, the words *offered to you* caught Marietta's eye.

> *I offered to you my heart, but you would not have it.*

She started to skip forward, but then came back.

> *I offered to you my heart, but you would not have it. Accept, then, my heart's blood. For Grandfather always said that earth was the*

*heart's blood of the Stottles. That was why we
left England, to have our own land. So now I
offer to you Wellhaven Plantation—my home,
my property, my heart's blood. I do not offer
this as a lure to entice you to my side, but as
a gift, freely given, for I am no longer happy
there, since I am without you. Accept it, with
or without me. The marble halls hold no more
charm for me, the rich delta soil—*

It started to get sentimental, and Marietta lost
patience. She turned to the last page. It was the
deed to Wellhaven, signed over to her, granting her
all rights and monies, now and forever.

"Oh my," she said, fanning herself.

She spotted Daniel Clarke standing with the
Eldridges. She spoke up loudly and clearly, as befit-
ted the mistress of a plantation. "Will Stottle has
just given me Wellhaven, as a token of his affec-
tion."

There was a murmur of surprise, sounding—
Marietta realized after a long moment of smiling
sweetly—more shocked than pleased.

"You can't possibly be thinking of accepting this
offer?" said Mr. Eldridge.

Marietta looked down her long, perfect nose at
him. "Why not?"

"Because the poor boy's wits are obviously
addled. Possibly the effect of the horrors he

witnessed in the war, and of coming back to find his father dead and his mother dying."

"And *my* effect on him," Marietta reminded, standing straight to emphasize her bosom.

Next to her, Mama said softly, disapprovingly, "It wouldn't be proper."

"Yes, it would." Marietta was shocked at the unexpected *attack* from her mother. She looked to Papa for support. "This will more than double our property," she reminded him.

But Papa, wearing a stern look, only shook his head, tight lipped.

"Well, he didn't give it to *you,*" Marietta said, "he gave it to *me.* Which makes *me* wealthier than *you.*" She tossed her head to make her golden hair sparkle in the sunshine.

And she caught sight of Daniel Clarke, who wore exactly the same expression Papa did.

What was the matter with everyone? She was young, and beautiful, and rich. Just the kind of person everybody loved.

But suddenly Will Stottle was there. His clothes were all wrinkled as though he'd slept in them, and his eyes were too bright, and he was smiling at her, looking much like a slave trying to escape a beating by acting all hopeful and meek. "Is it enough, Marietta?" he asked. "Is it enough to make you love me?"

They were all pitying him, she realized. *He* was making *her* look bad in Daniel Clarke's eyes.

"Love you?" She practically spit. "Will Stottle, I despise you. I'd give anything to be rid of you."

She heard the collective gasp of those gathered in the square.

It didn't matter. She knew what she had to do.

"Girl, you back again?" Granny Orilla jumped off the upended crate on which she'd been standing to fix her cabin's tar paper roof. Her hair was black and shiny, and she looked not quite as old as Marietta's mother, possibly thirty-five or -six years old. "I swear I never met nobody so dissatisfied with everything."

"Will Stottle is ruining my life," Marietta said.

"You don't know nothing about ruined lives," Orilla told her.

"Take another year"—Marietta held out her hand—"and make him stop loving me."

"I see you burning bright with the fire of passion," Orilla said. It took a moment for Marietta to realize the old witch was repeating the same words she had said that first day.

"Not for Will!" Marietta shouted. "I can't live this way!"

Orilla sighed. "No, I suppose you can't." She took Marietta's hand. "The taking away of love," she said, "is a chancy thing. There's no telling—"

"Yes, yes," Marietta said. "Just do it."

Orilla did it.

That night Marietta awoke with Will Stottle's hand over her mouth.

He must have climbed the cherry tree and gotten in through her window, for in the moonlight she could see where his foot had come down on the curtain, ripping it from the rod.

Maybe Papa had heard him entering, she thought, and was even now coming down the hall to see what was the matter.

But she was in the very room, and *she* hadn't heard.

"Where is it?" Will hissed into her ear.

Leave it to Will to cover someone's mouth, then start asking questions.

Marietta made a move to swat his hand away, because he was beginning to hurt her, but he showed his other hand, the one that wasn't over her mouth: He had a knife.

She was frightened, a bit—but mostly she was very, very angry.

"Softly, now," he whispered, and slowly took his hand away from her mouth. "Where's the deed?"

"Changed your mind?" she asked softly but scornfully. "I thought I was the love of your life, your reason for being. I thought you gave me Wellhaven, whether I'd have you or not?"

"I don't know what possessed me," Will said. "I never cared for you. I need to see if Violet will have me back."

"After the spectacle you've made of yourself?" Marietta asked from between clenched teeth. "You'll never be able to show your face without everybody laughing. You'd best try to start new someplace else."

"Wellhaven is *my* land," Will said. "My grand-daddy—"

"The deed's in the nightstand drawer." Marietta pointed. "But everybody *knows* you gave it to me. Everybody *knows* I'd never give it back unless you threatened me. Think that's the kind of man Violet wants? One who shames her and breaks his word and threatens women?"

For a moment Marietta feared she'd gone too far. Will stood looming over her bed, and she realized that he *might* kill her. He might not be satisfied with retrieving the deed.

But then he opened the drawer she had pointed out. Should she try to escape, calling for help? He was only two steps away, and she didn't dare, knowing that might be the action to tip the balance. A moment later, he slipped his knife away. She heard the scrape of a match, and the oil lamp on her nightstand flared to life.

"It's the deed," she assured him, thinking that he suspected some trick, "the same deed you gave me."

"You're right," he said, and it took her a moment to realize he was answering what she'd said before, not what she'd just said. "It could never be the same."

Then he put the parchment to the flame.

"You fool!" she cried out.

With his free hand, he shoved her back down, then he dropped the burning paper onto her bed. "Yes," he agreed. He swung the lamp, flinging burning oil over the furniture, the floor, the bedcovers. And still he held her down, preventing her from scrambling away from the rapidly spreading fire.

"Papa!" Marietta screamed, but already the air shimmered from the heat, and already it was hard to breathe.

Will just sat there, holding her tight.

As the paddle wheeler went up the river, the passengers caught a glimpse of the burned-out shell that had been the DuChamps family home for three generations. Daniel Clarke shook his head at the terrible waste.

But then he turned his attention back to the charming and beautiful young Creole woman. "Much more opportunity in the North," he assured her, finishing the thought he'd started. "I'm sure you and your..." He hesitated, unsure—she was obviously too young to be the child's mother. "Sister?" he asked.

"Ceecee's closer to being my niece."

"I'm sure you and your niece will love Philadelphia," Daniel finished. He hesitated, not wanting to sound too forward, since they'd only just met. "But if you don't know anyone in Philadelphia, I'd welcome the opportunity to be your guide."

"How kind of you," Ceecee's aunt said. "May I repay you by telling your fortune?" She took his hand, then looked up, her dark eyes pleased and friendly. "Look"—she showed him where—"a nice, strong, *long* lifeline."

THE WITCH'S SON

1776—Summerfield, New York

WHEN ABIGAIL BREWSTER brought her son, Hugh, back from the dead the first time, he looked all fragile and wispy, like morning mist on the village commons.

She was so startled to see her magic actually work—though she had studied and planned the whole year for just this thing—that for long moments she could do nothing but silently gaze at him. His face was pale and she'd forgotten how young nineteen years old looked, but his expression was peaceful, which should have set her heart at ease.

Except that his blood was bright red against the white of his homespun shirt.

And there was so very much of it.

They'd had him buried before she got home, saying that he'd been killed by a single musket shot and that he'd died instantly. He hadn't suffered, Josiah Blodgett had assured her repeatedly: The deed over so quickly, Hugh had never known what was happening. But now Abigail saw that he'd been shot several times, and she feared that if the first part of what they'd said wasn't true, there was a good chance the second part had been a lie, too.

Anger and grief returned her voice to her. "Hugh," she whispered.

Still, he was already beginning to evaporate like the morning mist.

She reached out...

...and felt nothing...

...and by then he was gone.

The second anniversary of Hugh's death, Abigail adjusted the amounts of what she had boiling over the fire, and she made sure to gather all of the ingredients—not just the mandrake root—at midnight under a full moon.

Once again steam and vapor bubbled out of the pot, more than the heat and the ingredients could account for, and once again Hugh took shape in the cloud that formed in her kitchen.

"Hugh." She spoke sharply, and immediately, lest the spirit once again dissipate with the steam.

Abigail saw nothing to indicate Hugh was aware of his surroundings. His eyes were open but unmoving. Abigail couldn't tell if he was breathing, if his heart beat once again.

"Hugh," she called a second time, but already the steam was thinning out.

Had it lasted longer this time? Was the vision more solid? Abigail couldn't be sure. Next year she must be calmer; she must take careful note of what happened, which changes were beneficial, which had no effect. She must take her time, she scolded herself, even if she had to work with a year in between each step of the way, for the spell could only be done on October 18, the same day that he had died, and only after two-thirty in the afternoon, the hour he had died. *You won't get him back next year,* she told herself. *Or the year after, or the year after that.*

With that settled, she told herself: *So you must make each attempt count.*

The fifth year Abigail worked her spell, Hugh still didn't seem to see or hear her, but this time, just as the steam spread out—much too early, disturbed by a draft from under the door—she saw him blink.

The eighth year Hugh gazed about the room when she called his name, an unhurried, untroubled gazing, as though he heard her but was unable to identify her voice or where, exactly, it came from.

The tenth year his expression was more vague and dazed than previously and he didn't react at all to her voice, but the blood was gone, his shirt no longer tattered from musket shot.

The thirteenth year his body still free of the wounds that had killed him, Hugh looked instantly and directly at her when she called.

And recognized her, she was sure of it.

She stepped forward to hug him, forgetting he was just smoke and vapor, and felt *some*thing—like the memory of a touch—before he slipped away into nothingness.

Maybe next year, she told herself.

And cried every bit as much as she had the year he had died.

1789

For Hugh, coming back from the dead felt like waking slowly out of a fever dream. He was aware of himself, in a way that was somehow different from the way in which he'd been aware of himself up until then—different, yet familiar. He was drifting away from someplace he hadn't intended to leave, and he felt a moment of panic. There had been bright colors and feelings for which he no longer had names, and so they slipped away from him, like a dream where the more you try to remember, the more it's gone.

But there was brightness here, too, and sound, as though he was awakening long past daybreak, to a morning already half gone. He'd lived in the same

house all his life, but for a moment he was confused, unable to place where he was in relation to
doors and windows. His body was weak and ached
all over, and he thought he must be just getting
over a long illness. For some reason, he didn't know
why, he put his hand to his chest, but that didn't
hurt any more than the rest.

He heard his mother call his name, and he
turned to see her standing before him. In the moment it took to realize that he was standing, too,
and that they were in the kitchen—so he couldn't
have been awakening from his sickbed—in that
moment Hugh remembered dying.

He swayed and clutched at a chair, then let go
when he realized he was going to fall anyway and
he didn't want to bring the chair down with him.
In a moment Mother was there, putting her arm
around him, lowering him to the floor more gently
than he'd have made it on his own, and how could
that be if he was dead and she wasn't?

Hugh felt the solidness of her arm; he felt the
hard wooden floor under his knees, the heat from
the fireplace, and the cold from under the door. He
took a deep shuddering breath and was disconcert-
ingly aware that it was the first in a very long time.

Out on the street, Tessa Wakley passed in front
of Brewsters' Apothecary and saw that Abigail
Brewster had the door to the shop barred and the

house shutters closed. *I hope everything is all right,* Tessa thought at the unaccustomed lack of activity.

But then she realized the date. Though it was warm for late October, Tessa began to shiver.

And she began to remember, though she fought hard not to.

Fourteen years ago, Tessa was five. Seventeen-seventy-five had been a year of people shouting, that was her clearest impression. People who used to be friends spat at each other on the street. All the grown-ups were caught up in the debate: loyalty to England or independence. At the time she didn't understand what was meant when her parents said they were patriots and the Brewsters were loyalists. At five, she only knew there were certain of her friends that she was no longer allowed to play with, and certain people with whom her parents and their friends no longer did business. There would be no more going two doors down and getting cookies from Mrs. Brewster, her parents said.

Fourteen years ago today, Mr. and Mrs. Brewster were away visiting a sick relative. This worked out well for Tessa because now she wasn't exactly disobeying her parents' instruction not to visit Mrs. Brewster, and because whenever the Brewsters' son, Hugh, was in charge of the cookies, she'd get two instead of one. Also, Hugh let her sit on the tall stool behind the apothecary counter.

On this particular day, Hugh had opened the

door between the shop and the living area, for he was working at the kitchen table, going over the account books, which meant he was being too serious to be good company. After finishing her cookies and climbing up and down the stool four or five times, Tessa had just entered the kitchen to let Hugh know she was leaving when she heard the door to the apothecary open. Tessa turned and, for a moment, couldn't make sense of what she saw—sticks? thin metal pipes?—sticking through the doorway.

All in an instant, Hugh grabbed her arm, dragged her back, shoved her head down, and gave a hard push that sent her sprawling onto the floor behind the barrel of flour that stood between table and stove.

There was no time for outrage. Tessa heard four explosions, muskets being fired, and the air filled with smoke and the smell of burning powder. Hugh staggered backward, his hand to his chest, as blood seeped between his fingers.

Tessa backed away as far as she could, caught in the corner between barrel, stove, and wall.

Men came in, their boots loud on the wooden floor. Someone walked directly to where Tessa hid, shoving the flour barrel so that it tipped over.

She closed her eyes and covered her ears. But still she heard someone shout, "No!" And it sounded—Tessa hardly dared hope—like her father.

She opened her eyes and looked all the tall distance up to the face of someone she didn't recognize. Someone holding a musket.

A moment later her father pushed this man out of his way. "No," her father said again, forcefully.

She held her arms out and he picked her up, the way he would pick her up in the morning to bring her down to the table for breakfast. In a moment, she thought, her father would use that same forceful voice to tell them to leave Hugh Brewster alone, to get bandages for him.

For the men had forced Hugh to the floor. Josiah Blodgett had his foot against Hugh's chest, holding him down while the other two men reloaded their muskets. But her father said nothing.

"Daddy," she said, and he gently pushed her face into his chest—to quiet her, to prevent her from seeing any more than she'd seen.

He was carrying her out of the kitchen, out of the shop. How could he fail to see Hugh's danger? "Daddy," she repeated, but he told her, "Hush."

Out in the street, she heard the *crack* of their guns. She buried her face deeper yet into her father's chest, even knowing that at the same time he carried her, he also juggled his hunting rifle, the barrel warm against her leg from having just been fired.

That was what Tessa Wakley remembered about the day Hugh Brewster was killed.

So she didn't knock on Abigail Brewster's door.

Abigail sat on the chair—which was not a rocking chair—and rocked back and forth.

Hugh was making busywork for himself, fussing with the fire, which, Abigail estimated, didn't really need fussing over. But Hugh very obviously preferred not to look at her as yet. He remained crouched before the fire for a very long time, staring into the flames.

Abigail would have feared that being dead had affected the boy's mind, but Hugh had spoken. "Mother," he'd said, clasping her hand so tightly that in other circumstances it would have hurt, and "Here," as he'd helped her up off the floor and led her, stiff and tottery, to the chair, "sit down." As though he were speaking to one of the village grandmothers, she thought, before she remembered that now she was old enough to be his grandmother. But Hugh had always been a polite boy.

She became aware of her own rocking, and she willed herself to sit still, her hands clasped tightly in her lap.

It was, after all, Hugh who finally started. "How long?" he asked in a shaky whisper, finally looking up at her.

"Fourteen years," Abigail said.

That was obviously worse than he'd expected, no matter how old she looked. Hugh momentarily closed his eyes.

"Among your father's books of medicines," she said, "which were passed down to him by his father and his father before him, were very old papers. Recipes. Mixtures." There was no use mincing words. He knew it wasn't medicines that had brought him back. "Spells. This one could only work..." Her voice caught for a moment, and she finished, "...once a year."

Hugh accepted all that. He asked, instead of any of the other questions he could have asked, "Where *is* Father?"

"He died," she answered as gently as anyone could give that answer, "after surviving the war for independence, in a riding mishap."

Hugh wrapped his arms around himself. "Can you do"—Hugh couldn't find the words and gestured helplessly—"this," and she knew exactly what he meant—"for him?"

She shook her head.

"You brought *me* back."

"Because you died here," she said, the words slipping out of her painlessly after all. "I had your blood—" She didn't want to tell him how she and John had come home to find the body already removed, surprising Prudence Wakley on her hands and knees, crying and scrubbing at the bloodstains.

Abigail wasn't ready to say how she had saved that bucket of soapy bloody water, and how—when it was all used—she had pried the floorboards up and chipped the plaster from the walls. "I had your blood to work with," she said, "and the exact spot you died."

Hugh stood abruptly, looking sick—though you'd think a man more than a dozen years dead wouldn't be squeamish—looking as though he needed to get away. But there was no place to go, and he only turned his back on her.

"There's more," Abigail said, because there was no good time to say what she had to say, nor a good way to say it. "The men who..." She couldn't say the word.

"Josiah Blodgett," Hugh said in a voice little more than a whisper. "Archibald Godwin. Nick Bonner. Nathan Wakley."

Abigail nodded. It had been no secret. The act had been considered—not murder, but warfare. There had been no trials, no punishments. So far.

"Archibald Godwin and Nick Bonner were killed fighting during the Revolution," Abigail told Hugh. "Josiah Blodgett died of a fever two years ago. Nathan Wakley is still alive. And he's part of the spell that brought you back."

Hugh turned to face her again, looking as though he already suspected what she was about to say, although there was no way he could. He was just expecting the worst.

She gave it to him.

"This spell only works for today," she said. "At midnight you'll die again—unless you pay back those who did this to you."

Hugh had always known his mother as kind and gentle. Now he sat at the kitchen table and listened to her calculating the best way to kill a man.

She advocated a sneak attack, at night, breaking into Nathan Wakley's house and killing him in his bed before an alarm could be raised.

As she spoke, Hugh realized there was a tightness in his chest that didn't go away no matter how deeply he breathed. He determined not to take a breath, an experiment to see whether he really needed air, or if it was just a habit. A live man with enough determination not to breathe would eventually faint, he knew, and then his unconscious body would resume breathing for him. Hugh wondered if he was fully enough alive for these natural laws to apply to him: Would he eventually faint and—if he did—would his body take that breath? Or was that why Mother's spell had a time limit: Because eventually his body would require sleep, and if he slept, he wouldn't breathe, and if he didn't breathe, he would die, yet again?

Except, now that Hugh was thinking about it, he absolutely had to take a breath.

He realized, in that ragged intake of air, that the room was silent, that Mother was looking at him.

She had asked him a question, and he had no recollection of what it was.

"Hugh?" she asked, but Hugh had no idea how far she had gone without him, and he just shook his head.

Mother looked worried rather than impatient. "You have to kill Nathan Wakley," she said, going back to the very beginning.

"Are you sure?" Hugh protested. "Are you sure that's what the spell said?"

She rested her hand on the book that lay on the table. He had been vaguely aware of it, had seen it and assumed it was the Brewster family Bible. It was definitely *not* the Bible. Mother opened the volume and turned to the appropriate page. " 'Raising someone dead of another's violence,' " she read out loud.

The book was old, faintly musty, the parchment yellow, brittle, and thicker than the paper used by Gideon Bourcy's modern printing press in the office of the *Summerfield Observer*. This book was handwritten. Hugh, sitting across the table from his mother, viewed the text upside down. The letters were tall and skinny and unadorned, so that the words looked like clusters of long-legged spiders, and Hugh wouldn't have been too amazed to see them scurry off the page. But that might have been because of the guesses he made regarding the person who had written them.

Mother read out loud the advisories, the limitations, the preparations, the ingredients. The English was old-fashioned, obscure, but the ending seemed clear enough: " 'By the final stroke of midnight,' " Mother read, " 'the dead man must have repaid the doer of the deed, or he will sink once more and forever into the realm of the dead.' "

Even upside down, Hugh could make out those words, written in bold capitals: REALM OF THE DEAD.

Mother was watching him. Very softly, she asked, "What was it like?"

And in the hearing of those words, the last of it was gone around corners in his mind, so that he had to answer, in all honesty, "I can't remember." He added, "It was nothing bad." But his answer was based on little more than a fleeting impression, and a memory that, with Mother's spell pulling him back, he'd hesitated.

"Still," Mother said, sounding very afraid, "it must be better to be alive."

He wasn't sure how to answer, to cause her the least pain.

"I couldn't bear to lose you again," she whispered. "I've fought so long for this..."

"I like the idea of being alive," Hugh assured her.

Mother took a deep breath. "What else could 're-pay' mean," she asked, "besides killing the killers?"

"Most of them are dead already," Hugh reminded her. "Without me. Are the conditions already impossible to fulfill?"

"I don't know," Mother admitted.

"What if I killed a man for nothing?"

"Hugh," Mother said reasonably, "remember who these men are. Remember what they did."

Hugh didn't need to be told to remember. He wrapped his arms around himself, not for warmth.

"Fourteen years ago," Mother pointed out to Hugh, "it was four of them against one. Now, just as I master the spell, only one of them is left. Is that coincidence, or was it meant to be?"

"Don't," Hugh said, feeling that tightness in his chest despite the fact that he was breathing, and breathing hard, "don't bring the hand of God into this."

" 'An eye for an eye,' " Mother said. "A man is permitted to use deadly force to protect himself. If you can't do it, I will. But your scruples may condemn us both."

This was moving faster than Hugh could keep up with. "Tomorrow morning," he said, "when Wakley is dead, and I suddenly am not: What do you suppose everyone will make of this? How can they not know that we're responsible? How can they avoid calling you a witch?" Which were not, exactly, the questions that held him back.

"The town has carried this guilt for fourteen years," Mother said. "The war is over, and people are remembering how it was before. They will forgive us."

"I can't breathe," Hugh said, and headed for the door.

He heard the scrape of a chair on the floor and was brought back, instantly, to that other October 18, when he'd looked up to see the armed townsfolk crowding the apothecary door, and he'd pushed back on his own chair, knowing even then that there was no time, no way to escape. He turned away, leaning against the door for support so his mother wouldn't see how shaky he was. He managed to glare, and she sat down again without a word.

Outside, the afternoon was moving on to dusk. Hugh began walking, so that no one would start to wonder who he was, loitering about Brewsters' Apothecary.

It was too cold to be out here without a coat— surely that was something else that would attract attention—but it gave him an excuse to keep his head down, his arms wrapped about himself, and to walk quickly, as though oblivious to others. That, and the fading light, got him off the main street.

On back streets, after sundown, people were less likely to stare long enough to try to put a name to a face that at best was half familiar.

Summerfield had grown, very definitely had grown, in fourteen years, and had prospered, from what Hugh could see of it. He ran his fingertips along the bricks of a building where none had been before, to remember what bricks felt like, and when the building ended, he walked beside a picket fence, feeling that, too. He kept his mind intentionally blank, not thinking of what had happened, what his mother was depending on him to do, what might or might not happen afterward.

He found himself, by trying to avoid people, on the edge of the cemetery.

And at that point he could no longer keep his mind blank, and his knees did buckle under him.

Mother had said he'd been buried. He presumed in the cemetery, although that wasn't necessarily so, though—again—there was no reason he could think of that he should have been denied Christian burial. Given that it was no secret that he'd been killed, and by whom. Should he look for a marker, put up by his mother, or by the citizens of Summerfield: "Sorry, political emotions carried us away," perhaps?

She had told him, eventually, the specifics of the spell.

The knowledge that somewhere, probably

nearby, he had another body, that by now it would be decomposed down to a skeleton, that what felt like a body was no more than vapor formed from ingredients Mother had gathered in fields and chipped off the kitchen wall— He was suddenly finding it very difficult to get enough air. He clutched at his chest, unable to tell if the pain was from unfilled lungs, or musket balls, or Josiah Blodgett's foot on his chest.

With her head down against the stiff breeze, Tessa walked around a corner and saw she was coming up behind someone kneeling by the edge of the cemetery. A young man. And not at all dressed for the weather.

Evers's family plot first, she thought, trying to work her way back to which grave that must be, *then Goodwife Bellows . . .* She slowed her pace, not wanting to intrude, but curious—since there were no graves newer than two years along this edge— why such obviously heartfelt grief.

Unless the young man was not crying after all. He could be injured, she realized. Or, likeliest explanation at this hour, drunk.

Tessa slowed even more.

After running several errands, she was coming home much later than she'd anticipated. The sun had already set, her father and his apprentices were no doubt more than ready to eat, and Molly—that lazy girl who was supposed to help her in the kitchen—probably had not even started preparations for supper.

But there was nobody else around to help, if help were needed, and she couldn't bring herself to just cross the street and walk around him.

She came closer. "Are you well?" she was going to ask. "Do you need help?" But all she got out was "Are—"

The young man gave a ragged gasp and jerked around to face her with wide, startled eyes, indicating he had not heard her approach.

And no, Tessa realized in that second—*not just startled, frightened.*

"Are you hurt?" she asked.

He seemed to need to consider. "No." He sounded somewhat amazed, sounded as though he wasn't used to people being concerned about his well-being. Which was odd: Judging by his clothes, he came from a clean and respectable household. Merchant's son, she guessed, or journeyman to a master craftsman. And he was nicely enough featured that he no doubt had a good many girls vying for his attention, whatever his situation.

"I'm...fine," he told her. Already his voice was steadier, except that he had his hand to his chest, in a gesture that was familiar to her from the last year before her mother had died of consumption, never quite able to get enough air to fill her lungs.

But surely someone with consumption would know not to be out in the October night without a coat. "Thank you," he said softly, and it took a moment for her to trace that back to her asking after his health.

"Were you attacked?" she asked.

His eyes widened again at that, but he didn't answer, and she thought maybe he was a bit simple-minded.

"No coat," she explained her reasoning. "It's rather cold to be without one." She was getting cold herself, standing in the evening chill with a shawl that had been sufficient for the afternoon, but all he had was a thin shirt.

The young man shook his head, without a word. He wrapped his arms around himself, as though she'd reminded him that he *was* cold, and he stood, seeming steady enough on his feet.

"Do you need help?" Tessa asked. "My father's house is just down the way. You're welcome to warm yourself by our fire, share supper with us." She thought not to mention that supper had most likely not yet been started. "You could spend the night in the apprentices' room," she added, "if you need a place to stay."

Again that look of amazement. "That's very kind of you," he said with just the beginning of a shy smile, which she thought meant yes, but then he finished, "but I live only a little down this way."

He indicated vaguely and unconvincingly. "But thank you."

So very sweet.

Tessa wasn't sure she believed a word of this. She thought she knew by sight just about everybody in Summerfield, certainly everybody in this neighborhood, and she tried to place him, thinking there was something vaguely familiar about him and that he might be someone's younger brother. "What's your name?" she asked boldly. At nineteen she was something of an old maid, and old maids could be bold.

He hesitated. "Hugh."

No last name, and she could think of only one Hugh she had ever known, who this very obviously could not be.

"I'm Tessa," she said to this Hugh. "Nathan Wakley's daughter, at the bootery."

Hugh got that panicked look again, so that Tessa checked over her shoulder to make sure no danger was approaching.

"You *are* welcome at our house," she told him. "My father"—she hoped she wasn't offending him—"considers it his Christian duty to help whoever needs help."

Hugh was shivering uncontrollably. "My mother will be becoming worried," he told her, which had a certain ring of truth to it.

If he was going to refuse help, she wasn't going to be a busybody. "Take care, Hugh," she told him. In her experience, people named Hugh were not good at taking care of themselves.

He nodded once, tersely, and set off in the direction opposite from where she was headed.

She turned back, twice, but so far as she could tell, he did not.

Abigail was not interested in revenge. If she had simply wanted Nathan Wakley dead, she'd had fourteen years to accomplish that. But she was determined that Hugh would not lose his opportunity to live beyond midnight. She had just made up her mind that she would set things right with Wakley herself, when Hugh finally returned, shivering so from the cold that his teeth actually chattered.

"Fool," she told him, sitting him down on the stool directly in front of the fire. But she knelt to rub warmth into his hands and legs, and put a blanket around his shoulders. Then she tucked his coat—which she'd fetched from the chest in the attic, where she'd packed it all those years ago—in around his lap.

But he was watching her; she saw that he'd seen what else she'd fetched from the attic. Despite being neatly wrapped in soft felt, its long narrow shape gave it away: John's Pennsylvania rifle.

She saw Hugh's expression. His face said, *Let me be anywhere but here. Let me be doing anything but this.*

But he held out his hand, and took the rifle from her, and unwrapped it, and began checking it over, making sure—after years of storage—that it was cleaned and oiled and ready to use.

She and John had spent nineteen years raising Hugh to be gentle and decent and polite. She hoped the last fourteen years were enough to let him overcome that.

Long after he was warm, Hugh couldn't stop shivering.

"There's no other way," Mother assured him, which was the same conclusion he'd reached, or he'd have...What? Wandered off into the cold night rather than return home? His choices were definitely limited. He certainly couldn't have accepted Tessa Wakley's offer—much as he didn't want to kill anyone, he was most certainly not up to sitting to supper and after-supper small talk with a man who'd walked into his shop and, unprovoked, shot him at point-blank range.

Hugh tried to hold on to that thought: to remember the pain, the terror, the certain knowledge that he was about to die, the whoosh of undefinable sound and that incredible dizzying fall that had followed that second volley of shots. His breath caught for a moment, so that Mother gave another of her worried looks.

Hold on to the thought, Hugh told himself. *But don't share it with Nathan Wakley. Don't think of the terror he'll feel, or the pain.*

Or of his family.

Or of the fact that he might not be the same man he was fourteen years ago. *My father considers it his Christian duty to help whoever needs help,* Tessa Wakley had said. Penance? How many years of reparation were necessary to erase Hugh's death from Wakley's soul?

How many years before Wakley's death would be erased from Hugh's?

Except that—much as he didn't want the responsibility for Wakley's death—neither did he want to cause his own death. Dying—twice—in what felt like just a few hours' time was more than he could face.

Hugh looked up from his father's Pennsylvania rifle, satisfied—after the seventh or eighth checking of every inch, of every working part—that it was in working order and ready. The old flintlock took so long to reload, he was unlikely to get more than one chance. Still, he measured out gunpowder and wrapped, filled, and folded three paper cartridges, just in case.

He tried to blink away a mental picture of Wakley's daughter, Tessa, as she'd looked fourteen years ago, a child who used to come begging Mother's cookies. She'd grown into a sweet-faced young woman, Hugh thought, and kind-hearted, too: concerned for him, offering him, all unsuspecting of what he was, food and a place to stay. It didn't help to think of that.

Wakley's Boot Shop was only two doors away, though he'd walked three blocks out of his way to keep Tessa from seeing where he lived. Just past ten Hugh decided he needed to give himself time, in case anything went wrong. *What?* he thought. He knew he could never begin to guess the things that could go wrong or how to deal with a situation already out of control.

But he was having trouble breathing again, and even the cold was better than sitting here, waiting.

He got up abruptly.

At the door Mother adjusted the collar of his coat, tugged at the length of his sleeve. "Be careful," she begged, reluctant—he could well understand—to have him out of her sight. Once more she told him: "I couldn't bear to lose you again."

To which, of course, he had no answer.

Tessa still hadn't caught up to all the things she needed to do, even though it was long after the apprentices had gone up to the attic for bed. She was sitting at the kitchen table, mending the sleeve of one of her father's shirts, when her father came in from the workshop.

"Still up?" he asked, and—before she could answer: "You work too hard. Surely that can wait until tomorrow."

Tessa shrugged. Her father had no head for running a business or a household. She said, "But tomorrow there'll be other things that need doing."

Her father rested his big gentle hand on her head. "If there's always things that need doing, you shouldn't let yourself grow anxious over things that aren't done."

"Fine words from a man who's locked himself in his workshop all night," Tessa answered back. She bit the thread off at the sleeve and started on a button that was working itself loose. "Surely Seth Meeks can't be *that* eager for his new boots?" she asked.

Her father shook his head. "I'm just unaccountably restless." He poured himself a half tankard of ale and sat down.

Overtired, in Tessa's estimation. Two of the apprentices weren't working out, but her father didn't have the heart to dismiss them, for no one else was likely to take them on. Just as no one else was likely to ever want to hire or wed her supposed helper, cousin Molly, and they were likely to be stuck with her the rest of their lives. The trouble was, Tessa thought, her father was just too kind-hearted. Without Tessa to look out for him, he would be helpless.

But, coming on the thought of what day it was, she realized that wasn't exactly true.

She said, not quite knowing why, except that she was overtired, too, "Brewsters' Apothecary was closed and shuttered today."

Her father didn't need to pause to consider. "Fourteen years," he said. "Hugh Brewster would be older now than I was then." That was a thought to unsettle a person. Her father shook his head. "It was the right decision for that time," he said. "God have mercy, he was a danger to us all, and it was the right decision to kill him."

Tessa had heard this story, from more people than just her parents—how Hugh had been in a position to know things that could have gotten dozens of patriots killed.

Her father said—what she didn't need to hear because she remembered it well enough herself— "But I saw him push you to safety when he could have used you to shield himself. And that knowledge has haunted me every time I've closed my eyes since."

Terrible things happened in war, she knew—that had seemed to be the topic of four out of five of Pastor Greene's sermons all the years she was growing up—and she might just as well blame Hugh Brewster for having chosen the wrong side of the struggle, for choosing a side that in turn caused her father to make a choice that haunted him. She certainly owed more to her father, who had—to her, to everyone in the world besides Hugh Brewster— been the kindest, most generous person she knew.

But she also remembered Hugh pushing her out of the way.

She remembered how he'd stood, moments later, his hand to his chest, bleeding. Would he have had time—if he hadn't spent it on her—to duck, to evade the bullets? To escape?

Was Hugh Brewster dead because she'd been there?

"Maybe I *will* save this for tomorrow," Tessa said, setting the needle above the wobbly button.

"It's definitely past time everybody should be abed," her father agreed, staring into his tankard rather than looking at her.

Abigail sat in her kitchen, rocking in her chair that wasn't a rocking chair, and stared at the book that had told her how to bring Hugh back from the dead. Was it permitted, Abigail wondered, did it make sense for someone as deeply involved in witchcraft as she had become to pray? To pray for the death of one man, and the life of another?

The cold seemed to seep into Hugh's bones as he waited, hiding crouched between bushes and fence in the dark of the Wakleys' side yard. The knowledge that, really, after fourteen years his bones should be used to being out in the cold, did nothing to warm him.

Go to bed, he silently wished at whoever it was that was still astir, with lights peeking out through the chinks in the shutters of the workshop and what, by the placement of chimneys, must be the kitchen. There had been a light in the attic, too, presumably the apprentices' room. But that had been blown out shortly after Hugh arrived. Which might mean that the apprentices had gone to sleep. Or that somebody had gone up there and then come back down.

How many apprentices did Wakley keep? Hugh wondered. And were they boys or young men? And were they—or Wakley himself—likely to be working into the morning hours on some project that needed completing? These were all questions that he could have put to Tessa Wakley when he'd had the chance, if he'd been level-headed and practiced enough in deception to have thought of them.

A clock in the Wakleys' parlor chimed eleven times.

What if the time approached midnight, and the Wakley household was still up? Or, what if they *did* go to bed, then Hugh couldn't get the door open? Or, what if he did manage to break in without arousing everyone—would he be able, in the dark, to tell which was Nathan Wakley's room?

Too many things to consider, too many things that could go wrong.

If he thought about them too much, he wouldn't be able to move at all.

The lights in the workshop were extinguished, just as Hugh realized he could probably have done worse than to tap quietly but firmly at the bootery door and hope that Wakley would be the one who came to investigate.

After a few minutes a light appeared, briefly, in a second-floor window, then it, too, was blown out, leaving only the kitchen light on. Nathan Wakley, or Tessa? Or one of the apprentices? Or the hired girl Mother had said the Wakleys had taken on?

Hugh was very aware of the passing minutes. Mother's spell made him keenly attuned to exactly how much time he had left.

The light in the kitchen stayed on and stayed on.

Hugh blew on his fingers to warm them, shifted position to keep his legs from cramping. He tried not to picture Tessa coming awake at the sound of Father's Pennsylvania rifle discharging. Tessa running into the room. Tessa seeing her father dead.

Seeing *him* standing over her father's body. Come morning, if he succeeded, there could be no doubt in anybody's mind, so it seemed more honorable to stay rather than run, to try to explain... Would that make things better or worse for Tessa? He tried to put himself in her position and could not.

And still the light stayed on.

Hugh stood. In his spell-enhanced awareness of time, he knew that there were ten more minutes left till midnight. The time had run out for hoping to do this in the dark. He took several deep breaths, flexed his fingers. Realized he was just taking up time, still hoping.

He bit the end off one of the paper cartridges, poured the charge down the rifle barrel, and rammed ball and paper down on top. Then, without pause, he stepped up to the door and knocked, not loud enough to rouse the house, but to clearly identify himself as a visitor rather than a sneak thief. Hugh lifted the Pennsylvania rifle to his shoulder.

Nothing.

Hugh lowered the rifle long enough to knock a second time, more forcefully, then hastily raised it again.

"Door's open," Wakley's voice called out.

Any more noise and they were sure to have Tessa—if not the apprentices and maid, if not the *neighbors*—down here too soon.

Hugh weighed opening the door then hastily

raising the rifle and aiming and firing from the doorway, against actually entering. Certainly, the closer he was to his target, the less room there was for error: missing, or having a second person in the kitchen get between Hugh and Wakley.

At best, the rifle took a full minute to reload. Realistically, he would have only one shot.

Realistically, his hands were already shaking.

He swung the rifle around so that he was holding it—muzzle up, stock toward the ground—in his right hand. He hoped this would look less immediately threatening. He hoped he would still be able to move quickly when he judged the time right.

Hugh opened the door and walked into the kitchen.

Nathan Wakley was sitting at the table, an ale tankard in front of him. No weapon, Hugh noted. Nobody else in the room.

Hugh swung the Pennsylvania rifle up to his shoulder.

Against all expectation, against all reason, Wakley said, calmly, softly, "Hello, Hugh."

Hugh froze.

Wakley said: "I've been expecting you a long time."

The muzzle of the rifle wavered as Hugh's hands trembled, though Hugh told himself that Wakley must have run afoul of another Hugh, must have him confused with someone else.

It didn't make any difference. Hugh felt no inclination to take on the role of avenging angel. He didn't need for Wakley to understand what was happening or why. He didn't need, or want, Wakley's fear. He only needed to kill Wakley in order to live.

"It's all right," Wakley told him. "I understand."

But even as he spoke, there was the sound of bare feet hurrying down the stairs, and Tessa's worried voice calling, "Father?"

For the first time, Wakley looked afraid. He looked terrified. "Don't hurt her," he begged, a whisper so Tessa wouldn't hear. "She had nothing to do with it."

Hugh couldn't let the man die thinking his daughter was in danger. "I know that," he assured Wakley.

And at that moment Tessa entered the kitchen, wearing a nightdress over which she'd hastily thrown a shawl. "Is some—"

She stopped, seeing her father, seeing *him* standing just across the table from her father, pointing a rifle at him.

Then, proving he hadn't mistaken Hugh for someone else: "Tessa," Wakley said, as though the three of them had met at a spinning bee, "you remember Hugh Brewster. He and I have some unsettled business. Go back upstairs."

Tessa recognized him from that evening, Hugh

could tell. "Hugh *Brewster*?" she repeated numbly. She glanced from him to her father to the Pennsylvania rifle back to him. Suddenly her eyes widened, and Hugh knew she recognized him from much further back than this evening.

"Tessa, this doesn't concern you," Wakley said. "Go upstairs."

"No," Tessa answered.

There were only minutes left. Hugh could feel them slipping away. Still looking at Wakley over the rifle barrel, Hugh said to Wakley, "What do you mean, you've been expecting me?"

"You've haunted my dreams," Wakley said. "I thought you were a waking vision"—Wakley nodded to indicate the tankard of ale he'd been drinking—"except then Tessa wouldn't be able to see you." He considered a moment. "And I wouldn't have expected a ghost to have knocked." Another pause. "This is something of your mother's doing, I'm guessing."

Hugh took a steadying breath, knowing that not so very long ago people who had tried what Mother had done had been hung or stoned or burned at the stake. "There's no other way," he said so that Tessa wouldn't testify against her. "The only spell my mother could find to bring me back requires that I repay what was done to me." He was having trouble breathing again, which could have been fear, or the fact that his life was drawing close to an end. He only had about a minute and a half left to kill Wakley. He sighted down the rifle's barrel.

—and Wakley, nodding, said, "I'm sorry."

Hugh was able to drag in a ragged breath, then another. *"Why?"* he demanded shakily.

"We realized you'd learned about the weapons stored in Josiah Blodgett's barn. There was a British detachment heading toward Summerfield, and we were afraid you'd tell them about it, give them the names of the leaders of the rebellion."

"I wouldn't have done that," Hugh protested. He was shivering and spoke with his jaws clenched to keep his teeth from chattering. "I would have done nothing that would have gotten people killed."

Wakley nodded, but said, "There was no way for us to know that."

Seconds left. Hugh tightened his grip. "I'm sorry," he whispered.

"I understand," Wakley answered, the second time he'd said that.

Hugh tried to hold the rifle steady.

Wakley braced himself.

Tessa covered her mouth, but a soft cry escaped anyway.

Hugh felt the last seconds ticking away. All he had to do was tighten his finger the least bit, and he could live.

"It's all right," Wakley told him, no doubt worried that, the way Hugh was shaking, Hugh was likely to only wound him, that it would require reloading and multiple shots to kill him—the way it had taken with Hugh himself.

From the parlor Hugh could hear the first chime of the Wakleys' clock proclaiming midnight.

A sharp pain pierced his chest. *Now, or die*, he thought as the bell rang out a second time. If it wasn't already too late. Despite the pain he got the rifle steady.

...but couldn't inflict that pain on another.

The bell rang a third time, and Hugh let the rifle swivel to point downward. The pain was dizzying, and he dropped to his knees but managed to keep hold of the weapon, afraid that dropping it might cause it to discharge.

On the fourth ring he got the rifle safely set on the floor, wrapped his arms around himself to keep from crying out, and prepared to die.

On the fifth ringing of the mantel clock, Tessa realized what was happening: that her father was to live, and that Hugh Brewster was to die.

It isn't fair! she thought. *Why can't they both live?*

The bell rang a sixth time. She met her father's anguished look, and he shook his head helplessly. "I'm sorry," he whispered hoarsely.

A seventh ring.

Father was sorry, Hugh was sorry, everybody was sorry: Didn't that count for anything?

Eight...

Tessa rushed forward, to hastily kneel beside Hugh, to put her arms around him, to hold him close. She wasn't going to let him die alone a second time.

Nine...

There was a shadow at the open kitchen door. *"No!"* Abigail Brewster cried. Her shawl flapping around her so that she really *did* look like a witch, Mrs. Brewster ran into the kitchen and reached for Hugh's rifle on the floor.

Ten...

Hugh brought his hand down on the barrel. "Enough," he gasped. Tessa felt him shudder. "Enough."

Eleven...

Twelve.

Tessa tightened her grasp on him, not knowing what to expect.

Nothing happened.

He continued to breathe, somewhat raggedly, for another several seconds; but then he worked to bring his breathing under control. His face was drawn from the pain, but already he was beginning to get *some* color back.

Mrs. Brewster sank to her knees in front of

Hugh. "I'm sorry," she said. She looked in turn at Tessa and Tessa's father, repeating, "I'm sorry," then faced back to Hugh. "I thought there was only one way to pay back violence."

Tessa supposed this made more sense than it sounded like. She supposed it was the answer to one of the many questions that, eventually, would need to be asked. But for the moment she didn't have the energy to ask any of them.

Somehow—she doubted she'd ever learn exactly how or why—they'd all been given a second chance: her father, with his hand over his face; Hugh's mother, holding desperately on to Hugh's hand; Hugh, with his head lowered, obviously still too shaky to speak. And she herself.

She rested her head on Hugh's shoulder. Second chances didn't come to everyone. She hoped they would all do well with theirs.

AFTERWORD:
Where Do Ideas Come From?

PERHAPS THE QUESTION authors are asked most frequently is "Where do you get your ideas?"

The most honest answer I can give is, "Beats me."

When you're in school, teachers give assignments. They say: "Write about what you did on your summer vacation." Or, "Write a paper told from the viewpoint of your favorite vegetable." Some of the assignments are fun, and some are a burden. The good news is that when you're an author, there's no teacher to tell you your assignment. But the bad news is that when you're an author, there's no teacher to tell you your assignment. With the whole world to choose from, where does one begin?

So here's the second-most-honest answer I can give: Ideas are in the air all around us, and sometimes—when we're lucky—an idea comes along and smacks a writer on the side of the head and says, "Pay attention."

Curses, Inc.

This story is the result of being nearsighted.

I was in a restaurant that has a bulletin board where people can stick their business cards. As I was walking by, I saw a card that—at first glance—I thought said CURSES, INC. I went back for a second look and saw that what it actually said was CRUISES, INC. But I thought "Curses, Inc." was an intriguing business concept, not to mention a great title. With a title like that, of course I had to write about a modern witch, and what's more modern than computers and selling spells over the World Wide Web?

Skin Deep

"Skin Deep" came about because of a lunchtime conversation with some friends who are also writers.

One of the women, whom I had only known for two or three years, talked about being born with a birthmark on her face. She described being tormented by children, just as Ardda is in my story. Only recently had new developments in laser surgery allowed the birthmark to be removed. My friend said that this had changed her entire self-perception and—therefore—her life.

Talk about an idea smacking a particular writer on the side of the head: In this case, there were at least eight of us writers at that table, and—as far as I know—I'm the only one who came away with more than lunch. Perhaps this idea chose me because it knew I would be sympathetic, since I'd always felt like the ugly duckling who—instead of growing into a beautiful swan—grows into just another duck. I've always had mixed feelings about "The Ugly Duckling": I'm happy he's happy at the end—but, boy, do those other ducks get on my nerves.

PAST SUNSET

This was the first of the stories I wrote for this collection.

The idea started with a Halloween decoration a friend had draped over her doorway. From the street it appeared to be a beautiful lady dressed in white, almost like an angel guarding the door. But the closer I came, the spookier the face got.

I set the story in France, which is where my mother comes from. Parts of France are as modern as anything in the United States. But every once in a while you turn a corner and find yourself in an old section that looks even today pretty much as

I've described it, as though nothing has changed in hundreds of years.

"Past Sunset" was originally published in *Bruce Coville's Book of Spine Tinglers*.

To Converse with the Dumb Beasts

We have a cat. Many of our friends have dogs. For anyone who's ever honestly tried to guess what his or her pet is thinking, I need say no more.

Boy Witch

After I'd written all the other stories for this collection, my editor, Jane Yolen, pointed out that I had all kinds of witches—good-hearted, evil, beautiful, ugly, from several times past, and from today—but I didn't have one who was a boy.

I had a hard time with that. Though I know that during witch trials in Europe and North America, men as well as women were accused of and executed for being witches, I had a gender bias that made me think of witches as female. For two months I mumbled and complained and tried to come up with an idea that would fit a boy witch. Nothing. Finally I mentioned the problem to a friend. She didn't even need to pause to consider. "Why don't you write about a boy who's trying to be a witch, and his spells don't work?" she suggested—proving, once again, how story ideas can hit different people at random.

I started thinking how boys and men have a reputation for jumping into projects without reading the directions first, and there was my story.

Since Jane is responsible for "Boy Witch," I considered naming the girl who comes looking for a spell "Jane." But poor Emma goes through so much, I decided not to try Jane's sense of humor. (And the friend who gave me the idea wants you to know she isn't Emma, either; her name is Mary.)

LOST SOUL

This is the only story that wasn't written with this collection in mind.

Several years ago a friend wrote a story about a kelpie—a sea sprite who lures men to their deaths and sucks their souls. *His* story was a haunting tale about a kelpie who fought very hard against her nature, wanting to become human and never again harm anyone. It was a beautiful story, but it got me interested in writing about a kelpie who is very pleased with what she is.

I also struggled with the concept of losing one's soul, and I decided it meant acting in a way totally alien to one's nature—the way someone wholly lost to an obsession might.

"Lost Soul" was originally published in *A Wizard's Dozen*.

REMEMBER ME

This was one of the later stories I wrote for this collection.

I had already written "Past Sunset" in the first person (the story told by "I" rather than "he" or "she"), and I was concerned that this made it stick out too much and not fit in with the others. I needed another first-person story. Where "Past Sunset" is told by a narrator—Marianne—remembering what happened in her past, I decided that "Remember Me" should be written in present tense because the narrator has no past. I pictured him, standing confused on the road, and the whole story of why he had no past, and what would happen to him while he tried to find out who he was, and how the story would end—all this came to me in less time than it's just taken to describe it. All I had to do was type it, making this the easiest of these stories to write.

WITCH-HUNT

I wrote this for an anthology that was looking for "nightmare" stories. Editor Michael Stearns selected "Cypress Swamp Granny" instead, but I think "Witch-Hunt" is scarier. I think it's the scariest story I've ever written, because it's the most likely to come true.

I intentionally tried to mislead readers into believing that the story is set in a different place and time, to put a safe distance between you and Lyssa.

Until the end, of course. By then, you realize that—by reading this book—you're exactly the same kind of person as Lyssa. Better luck to you.

CYPRESS SWAMP GRANNY

Most of my stories start with an idea for the plot, or the characters, or some sort of central theme. This one started with the place.

About fifteen years before I wrote this, my husband and I visited New Orleans. While he was kept busy going to business meetings all day, I got to do tourist-type things: a trip down the Mississippi in a paddle-wheel boat, touring plantations, and walking in the city. *Someday,* I thought, *I'll have to write a story set here.*

As I said, that was fifteen years ago, which just goes to show that I can't be rushed.

"Cypress Swamp Granny" first appeared in *A Nightmare's Dozen.*

THE WITCH'S SON

This story started out with a moral dilemma, rather than with a situation or characters.

The law says a person may kill in self-defense—

that is, if one's life is threatened. I started wondering about this in a fantasy context: If it's all right to kill to *save* a life, is it all right to kill to *regain* a life?

Obviously the ending of "The Witch's Son" wouldn't work in a modern setting: Today, if Hugh Brewster returned to life after an absence of fourteen years, he'd run into all sorts of complications with birth and death records, Geraldo Rivera hounding him for an interview, and enough money owed in back taxes to make him wonder if it was all worth it.

Story ideas surround us, like a roomful of strangers at a party. Potentially, there are more possibilities than we could ever manage. But there are certain ones that don't interest us at all (like the kid who wants to tell you all about this science fair project on cats' hairballs), and there are others about which we instantly say to ourselves, "That one looks fun." Sometimes an idea—like a friendship— can seem interesting and full of possibilities at first, but the relationship doesn't go anywhere and eventually fizzles out. Sometimes an idea seeks us out and demands our attention and won't go away, and eventually we say, "All right. This might work out after all." And sometimes a project is like a blind date, like an editor saying, "I know what you can do. How about some nice author notes...."